Food Justice and Narrative Ethics

Also available from Bloomsbury

Concentration and Power in the Food System, Philip H. Howard
Food, Power, and Agency, edited by Jürgen Martschukat and Bryant Simon
Making Milk, edited by Mathilde Cohen and Yoriko Otomo

Food Justice and Narrative Ethics

Reading Stories for Ethical Awareness and Activism

Beth A. Dixon

BLOOMSBURY ACADEMIC
LONDON • NEW YORK • OXFORD • NEW DELHI • SYDNEY

BLOOMSBURY ACADEMIC
Bloomsbury Publishing Plc
50 Bedford Square, London, WC1B 3DP, UK
1385 Broadway, New York, NY 10018, USA

BLOOMSBURY, BLOOMSBURY ACADEMIC and the Diana logo are trademarks of Bloomsbury Publishing Plc

First published in Great Britain 2018

Cover design by Toby Way
Cover image: Volunteers of the nonprofit organization "Angeles Malaguenos de la Noche" (Night Angels of Malaga) share out food on Christmas Eve in Malaga on December 24, 2015. (© Jorge Guerrero/ AFP/ Getty Images)

A catalog record for this book is available from the Library of Congress.

Library of Congress Cataloging-in-Publication Data
Names: Dixon, B. A. (Beth A.), 1957– author.
Title: Food justice and narrative ethics : reading stories for ethical awareness and activism / Beth A. Dixon.
Description: 1 Edition. | New York : Bloomsbury Academic, [2018] | Includes bibliographical references and index.
Identifiers: LCCN 2018009302 | ISBN 9781350054547 (hardback) | ISBN 9781350054561 (ePUB) | ISBN 9781350054554 (epdf)
Subjects: LCSH: Food security. | Obesity–Social aspects. | Business ethics. | Mass media and culture. | Creative nonfiction.
Classification: LCC HD9000.5 .D59 2018 | DDC 363.8–dc23
LC record available at https://lccn.loc.gov/2018009302

ISBN: HB: 978-1-3500-5454-7
ePDF: 978-1-3500-5455-4
ePub: 978-1-3500-5456-1

Typeset by Newgen KnowledgeWorks Pvt. Ltd., Chennai, India
Printed and bound in Great Britain

To find out more about our authors and books visit www.bloomsbury.com and sign up for our newsletters.

For Mother, who has always been so proud of me
To Chuck, with all my heart
Thank you, Maggie, for herding me to the finish

Contents

Acknowledgments

I owe thanks to many people—students, conference participants, colleagues, and friends—who heard (endured) and commented on early versions of this work. Thank you especially to the following individuals, organizations, and institutions that created these opportunities: Society for Ethics Across the Curriculum; Poynter Center for the Study of Ethics and American Institutions at Indiana University; the graduate seminar on "Food, Choice, Freedom, and Politics" at Indiana University; the Department of Philosophy at Kwantlen Polytechnic University in Vancouver, British Columbia; the University of Vermont Food Systems Summit Conferences; the (Working) Food Group sponsored by the Department of Philosophy at the University of Vermont; and the staff at Mother Hubbard's Cupboard in Bloomington, Indiana. Also, I record my appreciation to students who enrolled in various iterations of my philosophy course, "Food Justice." Over the last six years I practiced these ideas in the classroom—sometimes to good effect, sometimes not.

I have used material here, in part, from some previously published works. I thank the publishers for permitting me to use revised versions of these earlier articles and chapters. Parts of Chapter 2 were published in an article titled "Ethical Rules and Particular Skills," *Childhood & Philosophy* vol. 11, no. 21 (January–June 2015), pp. 67–79. A lead article inspired the manuscript project, and sections from this article—published as "Learning to *See* Food Justice," *Agriculture and Human Values*, vol. 31, no. 2 (2014), pp. 175–84—appear in Chapter 3. Chapter 4 is based on material from "Rewriting the Call to Charity," *Journal of Agriculture, Food Systems, and Community Development* (2015), www.AgDevJournal.com. Finally, Chapter 6 draws on content from a book chapter titled "Obesity and Responsibility" in Anne Barnhill, Tyler Doggett, and Mark Budolfson, eds., *Oxford Handbook of Food Ethics* (Oxford: Oxford University Press, 2018), pp. 614–63.

Garden Journal: Ordering Seeds

Sometime in mid-February 2012 when the temperature in upstate New York hovered around 10 degrees, a bottle of Great Western Extra Dry Champagne appeared in our refrigerator. It stayed there for a few days begging to be opened. I eyed it right back. A similar bottle showed up last year around this time, so I knew what was coming. Not a celebration of something we accomplished necessarily. But something we were preparing to do; a plan that depended on organization, critical review, optimism, and warm weather. We uncorked the bottle, poured the bubbly, spread the seed catalog by Pine Tree Seed Company out on the coffee table, and proceeded to order the seeds for our vegetable garden. The champagne adds a festive touch to this event. The more we drink, the more likely it is that we will forget that we are still in the grip of winter, wearing bulky coats, gloves, and hats. It's like the champagne allows us to do some time-traveling into the future. "Yay! Here we are in May. The sun is actually warm, the patio table is set for outdoor dining, our feet are dirty from wearing sandals, and spinach and lettuce are poking up in the raised beds." This is what we imagine as we pore over the seed catalog, and pour more to drink.

Ordering seeds should be a careful review of last year's successes and failures, recorded in a small spiral notebook. However, sometimes we get less serious when we combine the planning of our garden with drinking champagne (as one might imagine). We do well at the start. But then a kind of goofiness sets in and we may order some seeds that we are surprised to see once the package is delivered. That happened this year when I added cinnamon basil to the order, knowing fully well that my proclivity to grow large amounts of basil was threatening our marriage.

Still, ordering the seeds is a turning point in winter. Even though we can't quite do anything with them when they arrive in the mail, the garden is at least a possibility by this time. A few more weeks and we'll bring the growing lights down from the attic. This artificial light will cast a weird glow to our living room until late at night. And it will sometimes wake us up too early when it is still pitch dark outside. That's okay. Seedlings and humans, alike, need a head-start on the growing season.

Introduction

Eight years ago my husband and I filled in our swimming pool with about 3–4 dump truck loads of sand, a concrete patio, a diving board, and four inches of topsoil. Since we were left with a landscape of sand and dirt, followed by mud, and (very quickly) weeds, we set about designing and creating a raised-bed garden. We now grow large quantities of vegetables. This was the beginning of my interest in food: growing it, cooking it, and ultimately finding ways to get rid of it. This activity was also my point of entry to issues about food justice.

There are many ethical issues that cluster around the term *food justice*. But I can delineate the intellectual terrain somewhat by following the usage of a few leaders of the food justice movement. Mark Winne (2008), author of *Closing the Food Gap: Resetting the Table in the Land of Plenty*, writes that an advocate for food justice is a person who is intolerant to such a wealthy nation harboring 36 million hungry and food-insecure Americans. The argument that our food system is unjust and unsustainable is made by examining how food is grown, distributed, and consumed—through historical analysis of programs to end poverty, the popular surge of farmer's markets, community gardens, and food banks, as well as public policy initiatives to address health-related problems like obesity and diabetes. The authors of *Food Justice*, Robert Gottlieb and Anupama Joshi (2010), define food justice as "ensuring that the benefits and risks of where, what, and how food is grown and produced, transported and distributed, and accessed and eaten are shared fairly" (p. 6). Their examination of this broad topic uses a "seed-to-table" approach by exploring food justice in the fields and on the farm, in urban and suburban settings where consumers attempt to access nutritious food in the arena of national food politics and in the global food system.

My approach to understanding the particulars of food justice builds on both of these wonderfully clear and comprehensive texts. But the reader should know that this book is not intended to be a survey of the wide variety of topics related to justice in the food system.[1] Here you will find neither, for example, a discussion of the ethics of factory farms, the effects of agribusiness on local food and food markets, nor a documentation of environmental injustices that impact the sustainability of land and water use (Singer and Mason 2006). The topics about food justice that are included as case studies reveal a sample of my own idiosyncratic interests: food insecurity, farmworkers and farm labor, and obesity. These case studies are meant only as representative illustrations of a narrative methodology that has broader application beyond the particular stories presented and discussed in later chapters.

The project I undertake illustrates how food justice issues can be understood as part of a more general strategy to cultivate a skillfulness to *see* what matters ethically. Aristotle (1999) called this "ethical perception," by which he meant that a person who has acquired moral virtue and practical wisdom will also have the capacity to *see* what is ethically salient about particular circumstances of the world. Professional philosophers have devoted a fair amount of impressive scholarship to explaining and interpreting Aristotle on ethical perception and practical wisdom, but what is missing from this literature is a philosophical translation manual. A manual of this kind is faithful to the philosophical insights scholars have articulated but also tries to use and apply these ideas in real-world circumstances. If a translation manual is successful, then it will helpfully illustrate the main ideas and insights that philosophers are discussing among themselves. So to this end I hope to popularize the concept of ethical perception.

In the applied setting of food justice, acquiring accurate ethical perception contributes to the gradual development of ethical skills and competence to identify and describe injustices in the food system. As I illustrate throughout the book, one mechanism for cultivating this kind of ethical expertise is by reading, watching, or (re)writing a certain kind of realistic story that I call a *food justice narrative*. A food justice narrative should meet a number of demands in order to help develop ethical skillfulness about how to recognize injustice in the food system. These conditions include particularity, accuracy, and emotional engagement. I will say more about these conditions in Chapter 1. But the main idea is that a food justice narrative profiles individual people, social groups, or communities that suffer injustice and aims to make visible why we should classify their circumstances as unjust. Here we explore a number of stories involving actual settings where food is grown, distributed, or accessed. These are stories about making food choices as consumers, about who is hungry and why; stories that personalize who is working in the fields to pick our food; and stories that explore the relation between obesity and moral responsibility. These stories display on their sleeves facts about the world that constrain choices, truncate moral agency, and limit opportunities to live well. Understanding and explaining these circumstances, I argue, is a part of seeing what matters ethically in the area of food justice. But food justice narratives also prepare the reader for collective activism. Learning to see what is unjust in a particular situation positions the reader to more accurately identify what policies, laws, and structural conditions should change in order to discharge our responsibility for achieving social justice. How to practice this kind of collective activism is the subject of Chapter 7.

Narrative ethics

At the outset it may be helpful to situate the methodology I am using within the broader genus of philosophical literature, sometimes referred to as "narrative ethics." Nelson (2001) helpfully explains this kind of approach in ethics by identifying four questions that should be answered by anyone interested in using narratives to inform the moral life (Meyers 2004). These are questions about:

- *Narrative act*—what is done with the story?
- *Genre*—with what kind of story is it done?
- *Narrative agent*—who does something with the story?
- *Moral purpose*—why is this done?

In this section I answer the four questions Nelson poses while clarifying how my use of narratives avoids the criticisms she makes about similar approaches.

Here I use narrative as an educational tool for cultivating ethical perception. In this most general characterization, I am in good company since other philosophers have undertaken the same kind of project by employing narratives to "enhance moral perception," "motivate morally good action," and "guide morally good action" (Nelson 2001, 36). The main idea is that narratives are best employed in order to present what is particular and concrete about persons and their situations. When a narrative portrays these contextual details, we are better positioned to make accurate moral appraisals about the content of what we read or watch, as well as to engage our emotions in ways that educate and shape these moral appraisals. The purpose of narratives, as I use them here, is to reveal the ethically relevant circumstances that contextualize how individual people live as well as the background conditions that impede or constrain their actions. The content of what is disclosed by the narrative contributes to more accurate moral appraisals of actual people and what they can or cannot do, and why. So the narrative act, or what is done with the story, is to develop in the reader or viewer sensitivity to the ethical dimensions of living for ourselves and others or, as Nussbaum (1990) puts it, "to become more finely aware and richly responsible" (p. 148). While this heightened sensitivity is a moral good in its own right, it also ideally has a motivational dimension that inspires the moral agent to action, and further guides her to act in ways that are morally appropriate.[2]

What kinds of narratives satisfy these conditions? Nussbaum maintains that "serious" literary fiction has the capacity to direct the reader to the "subtle particulars of the narrative—the moral, intellectual, emotional, and social nuances … which are set out by the author with skill and imagination" (p. 148). But this leads to Nelson's concern about how we choose the books to read in order to enhance ethical perception. Nelson worries that many readers may not have the "narrative competence" to choose literature that meets the standard for being "good" or "great" in the sense described. In addition, readers must have sufficient "normative competence" to identify what literature actually contributes to ethical perception rather than corrupting these ethical sensitivities.[3] As Nelson suggests, it might turn out that even if a reader can discern what counts as great literature where she does possess narrative competence and can understand and appreciate the aesthetic features of these works, it is still possible that what she reads may fail to be morally edifying. In other words, choosing to read a work for its aesthetic qualities does not necessarily mean that it will contribute to enhancing ethical perception (Nelson 2001, 44).

The way in which I employ narratives avoids this difficulty raised by Nelson. First, I do not claim that novels or fiction, especially, enhance a capacity to see what matters ethically. Rather, I profile the educative function of realistic narratives: ethnographies, documentary films, memoirs, and real-world case studies within the particular content area of food. By drawing attention to certain essential features of these narratives, the reader can observe *how* they can be used to cultivate ethical expertise in learning to see and describe food justice. So as a matter of practical consequence, the reader learns what counts as a food justice narrative and why, and how to go on to identify new examples of food justice narratives or to construct altogether new cases that satisfy the conditions I identify and illustrate in the following chapters.

This approach also circumvents a different criticism Nelson articulates about Nussbaum's narrative methodology. Nelson reminds us that not everyone has the kind of access to literature of the sort that Nussbaum believes can function to enhance moral perception. There are many among us who may never acquire the desire or ability to read sophisticated literature because "the material conditions, institutions, training, and experiences that would allow serious fiction to enter their lives are simply not available" (Nelson 2001, 44). Here again my use of narratives cannot be faulted for this reason. The kinds of stories I profile are popular readings and films accessible in the public domain. These are the stories that I urge my students to read and watch, being mindful that sustaining their interest and enthusiasm for the topic depends on using emotionally engaging and well-crafted documentaries, memoirs, or case studies to explore food justice issues.

Who is the *narrative agent*? Or, as Nelson asks, "Who does something with the story?" In Chapter 2 I use the expression "ethical novice" to signal that both children and adults at various stages of intellectual and emotional development can benefit from acquiring the skill to learn how to see what matters ethically about particular and concrete situations. Different food justice narratives may target different populations of learners. But for my purposes, the ethical novice is anyone who wants to acquire ethical skillfulness about what food justice is by reading and viewing narratives that point her in that direction. This also answers the last question Nelson identifies about *moral purpose*, or why this narrative methodology is employed. To *see* what counts as food justice (or injustice) requires a certain attention to particular features of the realistic narrative. These may be previously hidden contexts or circumstances that reveal, for example, who suffers from food insecurity and why, or what forces shape the choices and actions of migrant farmworkers, or what it means to be morally responsible for one's condition of obesity. The *moral purpose* of reading, thinking, and feeling about food justice narratives is to position oneself as an agent of change—to act in ways that aim to correct injustices that afflict those who are disproportionately affected in food systems.

This particular relationship between narratives and ethical action answers a final concern that Nelson raises about Nussbaum's narrative methodology. Nelson wonders whether or not a reader can move easily from reading novels and focusing on the particular psychological lives of fictional characters to the real world in order to recognize societal failings, institutional flaws, and ultimately act on behalf of justice (Nelson 2001, 45–6). This is an advantage of the narrative methodology I recommend here. Because the narratives I profile are about real-world situations and people, it is likely that the narrative will morally educate by focusing the ethical lens more accurately on existing injustice, unfairness, and inequality. Seeing, feeling, and understanding these conditions about the lives of those depicted in the narrative is actually the setting for activism. Consequently there is less distance between the skillfulness needed to read a food justice narrative and the skillfulness needed to act on behalf of food justice.

Master narratives and counterstories

Throughout this study I make extensive use of a philosophical concept that Nelson (2001) calls a *counterstory*. I extrapolate from Nelson's original articulation of what a counterstory is and how it functions, to suit my own interests in food justice. There are a few essential characteristics of these kinds of narratives that make this concept ideal for explaining the nature of injustices in the food system.

Nelson (2001, 6) characterizes *master narratives* as "stories found lying about in our culture that serve as summaries of socially shared understandings … often archetypal, consisting of stock plots and readily recognizable character types" that we use to make sense of our experiences and which inform our moral intuitions. In some cases master narratives may contribute to the oppression of individual people or the groups to which they belong by damaging the identity of those people whose lives are depicted in the master narrative. One of the ways in which oppressive master narratives can damage identities is by "deprivation of opportunity." This is the result when the master narrative imposes a degrading identity on a person or a group, characterizing them as morally subnormal or abnormal. For example, stories or anecdotes about women as the kinds of beings who are solely emotional rather than rational may contribute to regarding women as less capable in academic professions, and may result in depriving women from the opportunity to excel in areas such as math, science, or philosophy.

Nelson describes a *counterstory* as a narrative that is about individual or group identity as it is articulated by those whose identities are damaged. More specifically, a counterstory repairs the identity of those who have been oppressed by cultural ideologies depicted in master narratives. A counterstory functions to resist and respond to oppressive master narratives that deprive individuals and social groups of opportunities to live well. By doing so it contributes in a positive way to repairing oppressive identities by replacing damaging narratives with ones that command respect. In this way counterstories function not only to repair damaged identities by correcting faulty depictions of individuals or social groups, but they also aim to restore freedom of agency by casting these individuals as morally competent and deserving of respect (Nelson 2001, 151).

Nelson's use of counterstories to repair damaged identities proceeds in two steps. The first step is to identify what parts of the master narrative misrepresent persons and situations. The second step involves a retelling of the story to make visible the morally salient details of the master narrative that were suppressed. Because counterstories respond to particular master narratives, there is no "one size fits all" in constructing a good counterstory. This means that in order for a counterstory to function as a form of resistance to oppressive ideologies, we need to know the details about how and why a particular master narrative deprives individuals or social groups of opportunities to live well. As we will see in later chapters, master narratives about food create a kind of epistemic opacity about structural injustices specifically.

My use of counterstories diverges from the way in which Nelson describes and uses these kinds of stories. Nelson's answer to the question, "Who tells the counterstory?" is that the story is told by those whose identities are damaged by oppressive master narratives. In this way counterstories are "identity-constituting" and play an important role in self-understanding within a social group, as well as a declaration about "who we are" in the public domain. But a good counterstory that successfully resists the depiction of individuals or social groups as morally undesirable can also be told by a person or group whose identities are not impugned (Nelson 2001, 20). These will not necessarily be self-defining in the way described above, but these kinds of stories may still function to challenge the details of an oppressive master narrative. Most of the examples that I discuss in what follows are counterstories of this latter type. These do not always or necessarily recast the identities of individuals or groups, but they do conform to the other main characteristics of counterstories that Nelson describes. The counterstories that I employ, for example, stand in a necessary relationship to ethically damaging master narratives where this relationship is to resist the master narrative to some varying degree (p. 157). And, some of the master narratives about food that I describe are, in fact, generated by oppressive forces within an abusive power system that depicts individuals or social groups as morally defective (p. 155), or whose identities are merely absent altogether. The counterstories I use function to resist these narratives by rewriting the ethically damaging story. In particular, the examples of counterstories I use in the context of food justice aim for a more accurate conception of moral agency that captures the lived experiences and contextual background conditions of those who attempt to nourish themselves. In a similar way Nelson describes how a counterstory can repair damaged identities by setting out to *free the moral agency of the people it depicts* (p. 155).

It might be helpful at this stage to introduce by example the main themes of master narrative and counterstory. Here is one way of thinking about these ideas. Michael Pollan (2008) supplies an eloquent rationale for eating nutritious real food as well as a pithy set of guidelines for how to do so. To identify the foods that we should be consuming, Pollan recommends, for example, avoiding foods whose ingredients are unrecognizable and difficult to pronounce, as well as those that make excessive health claims. He suggests that we shop the periphery of grocery stores or avoid grocery stores altogether by shopping at farmers' markets. He encourages us to eat mostly plants and leaves, food grown from healthy soils, those that are in season (freezing them for use later in the year), and to drink wine with dinner. Throughout Pollan's "eater's manifesto" about what humans should eat to be maximally healthy, there lurks the assumption that we can freely choose to change our diets and the way we eat. Undoubtedly for many of us this is true. For a particular audience Pollan's writings are thoroughly inspiring and feasible. But what I wish to draw attention to here is the master narrative that operates not only in Pollan's work but also in many popular and informative documentaries about food. In this case the narrative script might be articulated in the following way. What food consumers need is more knowledge about the food we eat: where it comes from, how it is grown, and the harmful impacts of industrialized food on our health and the environment. Once this additional information is acquired, we can freely choose to change our diets or not. We are free agents in this respect. While I use Pollan as representative of this position, it is easy enough to find similar views articulated in other writings and documentary films about food, including *Food, Inc.* (Kenner 2008), *King Corn* (A. Wolf 2007), *Food Fight* (Taylor 2008), and *Ingredients* (Bates 2009). In these films, for example, we hear the following language: "We do have choices"; "It's a choice we have to make"; "You can make a difference in this world by being more demanding"; "Support local farmers"; "Vote with your forks, three votes a day."[4]

These narratives are incomplete because they leave out the actual people who are attempting to implement the "eater's manifesto" and the relevant details about constraints on free agency that are created by particular lived circumstances. Why does this matter? This master narrative does not actively create a degrading identity for individuals or subgroups. What it does do is create a vacuum of identity by failing to describe the lived experiences of those who attempt to nourish themselves. In this way, the default position, and the prevailing popular opinion, may be that every person has equal access to nutritious food. All we need is knowledge about what is good to eat and why. This claim is categorically false. But unless we see how choices about food are constrained we may not be in a position to correct these obstacles to free agency with respect to choices about food. And this would count as a deprivation of opportunity to nourish oneself.[5]

As part of the explanatory work they do, food justice narratives feature particular people or the social groups to which they belong and disclose the obstacles they face in implementing the choices that Pollan and other food writers recommend. These narratives illustrate that knowledge of how to eat is not always sufficient for choosing to eat differently than we do. The kinds of circumstances that constrain the freedom to eat nutritious food include, for example, lack of money, lack of time, no transportation, no accessible place to shop, diminished physical mobility, or ineffectual public policy at the local, state, federal, or global levels. By identifying constraints on free agency, food justice narratives are crucial for illustrating the concrete details of living that are in danger of escaping our notice. Once this context and relevant background information is included we are in a position to see how this person (or group), in this set of circumstances, is impeded in her access to nutritious food. This is not a question we are likely to consider if we leave out the identity of food consumers. My answer to the question about why we should cultivate ethical perception about food justice is that we need to identify and describe counterstories that correct the way in which master narratives implicitly disguise the identities and background circumstances of those who seek to nourish themselves.[6]

One fundamental mistake I identify in some master narratives we tell about our food system is a disproportionate emphasis on an individual person, stripped of particular background details and circumstances. If so, then a central way of correcting this mistake is by using a story that situates individual people in a context that more accurately represents the lived experience of our complex relationships with food. What the food justice narratives described here have in common is a focus on the situated agency displayed by *particular* lives—those individuals who are food-insecure, those who labor in the fields to pick our food, and those who struggle with obesity. These stories alert the reader to more *general* conditions. Consider the way in which Lorraine Code (1987) describes how this vantage point is achieved.

> The claim that literature is a source of knowledge rests upon a belief in the value of understanding the particular. It implies that a minute and inward understanding of particulars has the capacity to go beyond itself, to show something more general about certain ways of being and kinds of situations. The technique involved is the converse of Plato's technique in the *Republic*, where we see virtue "writ large." It is like a move in the opposite direction, from microcosm to macrocosm; it finds philosophical expression in Aristotle's view … that the

> proper approach to essence is through knowledge of individuals—that one comes to know whiteness through knowing this or that particular whiteness.

And what do we come to know about the "essence" of food justice by looking beyond the particulars displayed throughout these chapters? I have recommended adjusting the ethical lens to more accurately focus on structural injustice and oppression—conditions that constrain choices and create deprivation of opportunities for populations of people who occupy a social and political location in our food system. As I am using this idea, structural injustices create conditions of vulnerability for individuals and the subgroups to which they belong, while simultaneously creating advantages for other populations. Part of the need for food justice narratives is that structures are hard to see since, as Young (2011) explains,

> we do not experience particular institutions, particular material facts, or particular rules as themselves the source of constraint; the constraint occurs through the joint action of individuals within institutions and given physical conditions as they affect our possibilities. Marilyn Frye (1983) aptly likens this form of constraint to a birdcage. Looked at one by one, no wire is capable of preventing a bird from flying. It is the joint relationship of the wires that prevents flight.

But once we see injustice, what then? What is the *moral purpose* of a food justice narrative beyond revealing these background conditions? Focusing the ethical lens more accurately on existing injustice, unfairness, and inequality allows the reader to see, feel, and understand the conditions that affect the lives of those depicted in the narrative. And to answer the question about moral purpose, this epistemic vantage point is ideal for undertaking food justice activism.

One disclaimer about the ethical role of counterstories is necessary. While counterstories function to correct the ethical damage created by some master narratives, they do not guarantee ethical truth. In other words, some readers of counterstories may persist in holding their moral beliefs constant in spite of what they read. Or they may read a counterstory rather radically to support their own idiosyncratic interpretation. While these are possibilities, they do not detract from the primary ethical and epistemic purpose of such narratives. The job of counterstories is to depict the world from the point of view of marginalized populations—those whose voices are muted or absent altogether. Revealed are the particular details of living that include a person's psychology and the emotional texture of a life which speaks to what it means to be food-insecure, to live in poverty, or to work one's body to exhaustion in fields picking our food. The point of view illustrated by these kinds of stories is not ethically unassailable, leading the reader to one particular moral conclusion. Instead these stories position us epistemically to challenge master narratives that falsify or misrepresent these real circumstances. Nelson (2001, 67) remarks,

> [Counterstories] operate on the supposition that the norms of the community are to be found not only in its foundational narratives, but also in stories that offer other vantage points from which to assess a community's social practices. The teller of a counterstory is bound to draw on the moral concepts found in the master narratives of her tradition, since these played a key role in her moral formation regardless of how problematic her place within that tradition has been, but she isn't restricted to just those concepts. To the extent that her experiences of life and considered judgments make them available, she can also help herself to alternative understandings of lying, heroism, fairness, or propriety, testing her conceptions of these things for adequacy against conceptions offered by people within both her found communities and her communities of choice. The narrative agent who tells counterstories thus commands a wider range of moral resources [for those] who are unjustly subordinated or excluded by a community's foundational narratives.

So counterstories position the reader epistemically to take up a point of view that is not always clearly accessible. But the food justice narratives that I recommend as counterstories in later chapters have additional credentials that contribute to their reliability as guides to seeing what matters ethically. As I explain in Chapter 1, food justice narratives conform to the following three conditions: particularity, accuracy, and emotional engagement. We are less likely to make mistakes about how public policies or laws affect individuals and social groups when we can hear the particular voices of those who are directly impacted by these policies or laws, and when we are emotionally engaged by those who speak about their circumstances of living. Perhaps most importantly for assessing the ethical trustworthiness of food justice narratives is acquiring the skill to accurately classify particular circumstances as injustices of one kind or another: structural injustice, oppression, cases of misrecognition, or as impediments to political participation. Developing the skill to accurately catalogue a particular state of affairs under a more general moral concept is ideally acquired by attention to particular case studies. In Chapter 2, "Developing Narrative Skill," I explain how attention to these particulars contributes to becoming more adept at recognizing what ethically salient features of stories are shared across contexts.

Justice and injustice

The reader who is interested in food *justice* may expect some help defining what justice is. This is a reasonable expectation even though surveying philosophical theories about justice goes well beyond the project I undertake (e.g., Brighouse 2004). Nonetheless, I can describe how the narrative methodology used here intersects with some concepts of justice. As we will see in later chapters, food justice narratives are particular stories that include details about individuals and the social groups to which they belong. These stories often reveal constraints on choice owed to structural conditions. Or the story may position us to see what counts as exploitation or what it means to be marginalized, or powerless. In other words, the story facilitates in the reader the skill to classify a particular case under a more general ethical concept such as structural injustice or oppression, for example. So the methodology I employ is contextually defined by application to a particular case study.

The analysis of different case studies will surely lend themselves to different philosophical concepts of justice. For example, some food justice narratives may profile how marginalized communities lack the right of entry to political participation. In these cases the relevant philosophical concepts of justice that can be used to classify these circumstances as unjust are participation and recognition (see Fraser 1998; Schlosberg 2007). In other stories what may be revealed by the narrative is how governments and global trade agreements disadvantage local communities in their use of sustainable land, thereby impeding the livelihood of farmers. If so, the food justice lens should invoke the concept of food sovereignty ("Declaration of Nyeleni" 2007) or the right to healthy food produced by sustainable methods (see Holt-Giménez 2011a, 2011b).[7] Consequently, we should look into the individual narratives discussed in Chapters 4, 5, and 6 in order to understand how these concepts of (in)justice are introduced and used.

The food justice narratives presented in Chapter 4 are stories about individual people and social groups who suffer from food insecurity. These stories profile the structural background conditions that contribute to being food-insecure. So in this narrative context I urge the reader to focus specifically on identifying what counts as a structural condition, and how these conditions combine to create structural injustice. By using Young's (2011) account of structural injustice we can characterize this idea as constraining choices and limiting opportunities for those who occupy a social and political location, through no fault of their own. In Chapter 5 the food justice narratives I analyze are about farmworkers. In these case studies the new concept of justice introduced is oppression (Frye 1983; Nelson 2001, 108–12). This includes several different overlapping senses of oppression: marginalization, powerlessness, exploitation, cultural imperialism, and violence. What these various "faces of oppression" have in common is that they apply to members of social subgroups, restricting their moral agency, diminishing the integrity of and respect owed to that social group, and depriving its members of opportunities to live well. Chapter 6 focuses on food justice narratives that challenge the moral presumption that all obese individuals can freely choose what and how much to eat. The main philosophical concept I introduce and apply to real-world case studies is a theory of moral responsibility by Vargas (2013a). This account invites a closer analysis of how volitional control is exercised by agents. What is relevant to judging whether or not obese individuals are morally responsible for their condition is determining what structural conditions constrain food choices beyond what can be controlled by the agent herself.

What the reader may notice about the stories included here is that they profile *injustice*, rather than justice, in the food system. In this respect I follow Judith Shklar (1990) who reminds us that while justice occupies a central and prominent position in moral philosophy, injustice is neglected and even "shunned" in the theoretical literature. In order to correct this gap in our thinking, Shklar aims to give injustice its due by focusing on such questions as: What is the relation between misfortune and injustice? What events could have been avoided or mitigated? Who is the (collective or individual) agent responsible? And who is to blame? The stories that we read as food justice narratives invite exactly these kinds of questions. Crucially they inspire what Shklar (1990, 83) calls a "sense of injustice."

> When the victims of disasters refuse to resign themselves to their misfortunes and cry out in anger, we hear the voice of the sense of injustice. Voltaire is their poet. What, however, is the sense of injustice: First and foremost it is the special kind of anger we feel when we are denied promised benefits and when we do not get what we believe to be our due. It is the betrayal that we experience when others disappoint expectations that they have created in us … The sense of injustice is eminently political. In spite of all the difficulties of knowing how to tell an injustice from a misfortune and who the real victims are, we know perfectly well what we feel, once we do recognize them. When it asserts itself, the sense of injustice is unmistakable even when we refuse to acknowledge it.

Food justice narratives not only inspire a sense of injustice, they make possible a response to these circumstances. I do not mean to imply that by reading food justice narratives the reader comes away more personally ethical. Instead the ideal I recommend is collective activism that aims to transform bad laws that disadvantage the poor, public policies that create inequality, or institutions that degrade and disrespect those who are marginalized in our society.

Chapter summaries

Chapter 1, "Ethical Perception," introduces some main characteristics of the concept of ethical perception that will shape our understanding of how to use and apply this idea in the context of food justice. There are three main features of ethical perception that I identify and illustrate by example. First, ethical perception is what a moral agent understands when she notices what matters ethically about a *particular situation*. Second, the moral agent's perception is ideally graced by an *affective or emotional engagement* with other persons and the circumstances of their lives. And third, *accuracy* of ethical perception requires that the moral agent have a veridical grasp of facts about the world, as well as an ability to construe particular situations as instances of more general moral concepts like justice or fairness. There are two additional claims that I accept about ethical perception that may be more controversial. One is the idea that this kind of perception is constituted by a multiplicity of psychological states, processes, or skills, as opposed to a unitary faculty (as some have supposed). My view follows Blum (1994) in urging that ethical perception should be understood as a function of many psychological states and processes of the perceiver. If so, there are probably a number of ways to cultivate this kind of seeing. On my account, the strategies for cultivating ethical expertise about food justice may turn out to be just one kind of local and domain-specific competence. The second general claim that I endorse is that acquiring ethical perception is a developmental process. This characterization of the concept allows us to understand the cultivation of ethical perception as one that admits of degrees acquired in gradual stages. In this way we may regard any one of us as an "ethical novice"—someone who may want to incrementally improve her capacity to see what matters ethically in one domain or another.

In Chapter 2 titled "Developing Narrative Skill," I describe a methodology for acquiring ethical expertise by reading stories. This is not a methodology that exclusively targets children or even an account for those adults who have somehow missed out on the relevant kind of ethical instruction that the rest of us received about how to reason and act ethically. While I am especially interested in the start position for acquiring ethical expertise, and that does include children, this does not mean that most adults are done learning about how to appreciate the particular contexts and circumstances of ethical thinking, saying, and doing. So, the ethical novice is anyone who can benefit from improving their ethical life. That is probably most of us. What I recommend here is a skill model of practical activity for acquiring ethical expertise. I argue that these skills are not gained from the beginning by following rules or general principles. They are acquired by attention to the "subtle and complex features of situations." I illustrate how this kind of skillful practice may be facilitated by a certain kind of story that invites the reader to explore and reflect upon the ethically relevant contextual details of that story. To illustrate this point I have chosen Arnold Lobel's (1980) enchanting fable, "The Hippopotamus at Dinner." Employing a skill model of ethical expertise has broad implications for teaching and learning to be an ethical expert in a wide range of institutional and practical settings frequented by adults and children alike.

After discussing the general concept of ethical perception in Chapter 1, and the general skill model of ethical expertise in Chapter 2, the reader is prepared to apply these ideas to issues in the domain of food justice. I have said that food justice narratives resist and renovate damaging or oppressive master narratives about food. But we need to see specifically what these master narratives are and how they are damaging. In Chapter 3, "Food Insecurity: Hungry Women," I profile a representative sample of stories that describe who is hungry and why. These are real stories that can be found in the public domain—on the websites of some hunger relief organizations and some international nonprofit organizations that are devoted to improving the quality of life of those who live in poverty, lack sufficient food or clean water, or face obstacles to education and employment. However, when stories about hungry women, for example, describe the causes of hunger as owing to individual bad luck or accidental misfortune, then we may not see how a particular person's plight is produced by systemic injustices and broader failures of institutional inequalities. The damage done by this kind of story is that it disguises a solution to hunger that points to political justice rather than charity.

In Chapter 4, "Rewriting the Call to Charity," I explore a practical strategy for rewriting the very nature of what it means to engage in charity. Here I suggest how to rewrite stories about who is hungry and why by using particular case studies that I call *food justice narratives*. These counterstories profile particular people who are food-insecure, but they also include systemic background conditions that identify how groups of people are unfairly disadvantaged. Acquiring this point of view is necessary for undertaking our collective responsibilities for achieving food justice because it positions us to see what structural conditions must change. In this way food justice activism becomes a real goal, made possible by the creation of a knowledgeable and informed citizenry.

Chapter 5, "Farmworkers: 'It is Very Ugly Here,'" illustrates a case study about food justice in the fields. In his exceptional ethnography, anthropologist Seth Holmes (2013) shares his "participant observation" research about the Triqui migrant farmworkers. In his personal chronicle, Holmes discusses immigration, social and economic hierarchy, and health among the Triqui. These stories characterize a master narrative about migrant workers but they also convincingly resist this narrative. The testimony Holmes supplies from the inside makes particular and concrete the way in which the master narrative is damaging. In addition, Holmes also provides the attentive reader with analysis and commentary that shapes the basis for a food justice narrative—one that defies ideologies that falsely characterize reasons for labor migration in the first place, and which target and blame the farmworkers themselves for ill-health, oppressive working conditions, and poverty. The explanatory work of this food justice narrative is to challenge three main underlying assumptions: first, that indigenous Mexicans *voluntarily* migrate to work in the United States; second, that oppression is *natural*; and third, the assumption that individual *moral agency* always and everywhere operates freely of constraints.

As we learn, counterstories are a way of correcting a popular and prevalent "script" that individuals are *personally responsible* for eating healthy food, or that individual people are personally responsible for their "voluntary" choices to migrate to the United States, or that they are personally responsible for being poor. This theme about personal responsibility can also be detected in the discourse about the causes of obesity and proposed public policy recommendations that attempt to address the "obesity epidemic." In Chapter 6, "Obesity, Responsibility, and Situated Agency," I explore the moral sense of personal responsibility that characterizes much of the obesity discourse. Here what counts as a food justice narrative is getting the attributions of responsibility right according to some plausible theory of responsibility. To do so I employ Vargas's (2013a) *revisionist reasons* theory of moral responsibility. One conclusion of this analysis that is illustrated by the case studies included here is that we can better resist a popular misconception about obesity that targets obese individuals for moral disapproval and blame.

Seeing what matters ethically about a particular situation is a good in its own right. But it is also true that seeing well in this sense is crucial for knowing how to act and then performing the right action. Chapter 7, "Practicing Philosophy," explores this practical outcome of learning to see food justice. There is not one activity that I recommend. Rather, there are many possibilities for bringing our ethical expertise to fruition in the real world. The general demand is for social and political justice. Individuals may contribute to changing the politics of food by joining collective organizations that work toward this end. In this sense we are each responsible for justice.

Autobiography

My own foray into food justice did not begin with any ambitious or arcane objective. It began by starting a garden in my own backyard and by volunteering at a food shelf in Bloomington, Indiana, called *Mother Hubbard's Cupboard*. The small anecdotal stories about my experiences in these settings bookend the more theoretical philosophical analysis in each chapter. This will no doubt provide some relief to the reader. But the small stories are not mere accessories. In different ways these journal entries about my practical activities point to the same conclusion(s) that follow from the philosophical analysis. The idea is that targeting the politics of food by collective activism is necessary in order to discharge our responsibilities for food justice. Strangely, ordinary activities like gardening and volunteering open out in a natural way to include a concern about social and political conditions in local, national, or even global settings. I did not plan to align these practical activities with my philosophical conclusions. It seems that it just turned out that way. But what is possible for me may, by design, be achieved by others. Readers may benefit from my successes as well as the ways in which I fall short of seeing what matters ethically. In this style I hope to shift my relationship with the reader from being a *presumed* expert philosopher—"This is how you do it"—to "Hey, I tried. Maybe you (reader) can do better." So the methodology here is more like a travelogue. Traveling to particular places creates some familiarity with the geography. This familiarity of place is what I will pass on, and, perhaps, it can help others who are traveling in the same vicinity.

The main idea that I wish to convey through my own testimonials is to pay attention to what matters ethically about what you *do* as well as about what you *see*. To this ambitious undertaking we now turn. In what follows the reader may decide to do things differently than I have done. And this is what we should expect if what Aristotle says about acquiring complete virtue is true:

> This, then, is a sketch of the good; for, presumably, we must draw the outline first, and fill it in later. If the sketch is good, anyone, it seems can advance and articulate it, and in such cases time discovers more, or is a good partner in discovery. That is also how the crafts have improved, since anyone can add what is lacking [in the outline]. (*Nicomachean Ethics* 1098a 20–25)

Mother Hubbard's Cupboard: Meeting Mother Hubbard

On Monday afternoon a long line of people snaked out of a small office-turned-food pantry. Those in line were waiting with bags and boxes to pick up food distributed by an organization in Bloomington, Indiana, called Mother Hubbard's Cupboard (MHC). I was there to apply to be a volunteer, so I squeezed past some of these street people, mothers and children, and single men who were lined up patiently to enter the building. Inside it was a bit more chaotic. Food was coming off the shelf and into the bags of community members. There might have been five to seven volunteers helping to make this happen. Children were milling around as well, laughing and playing with some of the workers who seemed to know everyone they were serving. I was there to see Erin, who explained what jobs were available, what times they needed filled, and where to go. Since they wanted to know why I was there, I told them about my academic interest in food justice and how impressed I was by the work they were doing in Bloomington. One woman typing at a computer replied that they were all even more awesome in person! That inspired laughter all around. As I learned from their website, the mission of MHC is broad:

> *Mother Hubbard's Cupboard increases access to healthy food for all people in need in ways that cultivate dignity, self-sufficiency, and community.* ("What We Do," n.d.)

The food pantry is only one piece of this overall mission. In addition, a few employees supervise a contingent of volunteers who grow food in three community gardens, purchase and transport food from the large food bank distribution center, and engage in a multitude of educational activities in the local community to raise awareness about eating healthy food.

Since I arrived rather late in the growing season (October 9), there was not much produce coming out of the gardens. But the staff still needed help to clean up and close the gardens for the winter. So the next day I arrived at a MHC garden in the late afternoon to join about ten other volunteers for a two-hour work session pulling squash vines, digging out bind weed, and moving tools and supplies into a new shed that had been built on the property. Kendra was the staff member in charge of the garden work, and she immediately introduced herself and gave me a tour of the garden. I could see a few raised beds still producing kale, clumps of chives, vibrant strawberry plants, and peas with their vines looking pretty healthy. But since we had just had a light frost, the squash plants were ready to go to the compost, and the tomato remains were being bagged and thrown away because a fungus of some kind made them ineligible for the compost pile. The main problem, Kendra explained, was the aggressive weeds that had made their home alongside the crops over the summer. In particular, bind weed has a deep root with many offshoots, a skinny stem that breaks easily, and a propensity to grow anywhere and everywhere, choking the cultivated crop. So this is what we tried to take care of to save the future plants that would be trying to establish themselves next season.

Some of the younger volunteers were doing either high school or college service activity projects (one involving composting); Pam was interning in the garden as part of her master gardener apprentice program, and others seemed to have a long-term commitment to MHC. I met Anna pulling bind weed. She is an Indiana University (IU) student who has been volunteering at MHC since last March. I asked her why she was doing this work and how she got interested in it. She explained that as a high-school student she worked at a food shelf in Indianapolis, and then her interest in food began to point in the direction of asking who is getting food and who isn't. She began to do service activity projects with these questions in mind and eventually crafted an individualized major at IU that allowed her to combine courses in different disciplines that helped her define issues in the area of social justice and food.

I should mention also that as we were busy with the bind weed, a group of children aged 5–14 years ranged in and around the fenced garden. They were supplied with small colorful tools to fit their hands and small red wheelbarrows to push. They were busy, in a random kind of way, picking up mulch or compost and moving it around in the wheelbarrows—running, laughing, and chasing each other. I spoke with another volunteer later who said she had been recently hired as youth organizer. Her job is to provide some kind of organized gardening activity for the children who gravitate to the community garden. Most of these kids hail from the public housing project that is adjacent to the MHC community garden. And the produce grown here is primarily made available to this surrounding population (as opposed to being transported to the food pantry). The kids have their own section of the garden that they can cultivate. And, the youth organizer told me that there was one boy who had been doing just that for four to five years. Apparently he is here almost every day. The staff and volunteers knew him as well as most of the other kids who hung out with us. A few adults from the community work in the garden as well, and some enter to pick and eat the vegetables during the regular growing season. I wanted to ask whether the community requested the garden, or what they thought of it being established here. I guess I will get a chance to talk more when there are fewer weeds to pull.

The first day of volunteer work is about work, but it also seems to me it is more about meeting people who do this kind of thing.

1

Ethical Perception

In *The American Way of Eating*, Tracie McMillan (2012) is on a journey and we, the readers, are invited to tag along. McMillan's basic story involves going undercover as a journalist and finding a job in each of three stages of food: producing food, retailing food, and serving food. She picks garlic in the Central Valley of California, stocks the produce section of Walmart in Detroit, and expedites food plates leaving the kitchen of Applebee's in New York City. McMillan describes her discoveries as a kind of seeing that is novel to her; it is looking through a new lens that is directed on the landscape of food production, distribution, and consumption. This new way of seeing is available to the reader as well. McMillan (2012, 7, 13) says:

> The more I looked out on this vast landscape, the less I recognized any of it. And yet I couldn't stop looking, trying to figure out what had changed. Something had gotten under my skin and changed how I saw the world. And the first thing that I could recognize as truth in this strange new place was what I learned at Vanessa's side: Everyone wants good food … Eventually, I had to strip myself of it, and try to look at the world in a new way, asking the question, what would it take for us all to eat well?

I think this is the right question to ask but we may need to do some preliminary work as part of the inquiry. First, how best should we "try to look at the world in a new way"? What kinds of experiences or ways of seeing, thinking, and feeling will position each of us to acquire the kinds of insights about food that McMillan describes along the journey she takes from farm to table? My short answer to this question involves describing and illustrating how we may each cultivate ethical perception about food justice by reading stories about food.

In this chapter I introduce the concept of ethical perception in a way that I hope makes it accessible to a wide audience. I include Aristotle's own remarks about this idea as well as commentary by interpreters of Aristotle. These scholars are far better equipped than I to supply the exposition of the relevant passages in Aristotle. But what I hope to contribute to the already existing philosophical literature is an analysis of the concept of ethical perception that explains its role in the development of moral competence. In other words, I am interested in how ethical perception may be acquired and applied in practical settings in order to cultivate a sensitivity to what is ethically salient about particular situations that fall within the domain of food justice.

The concept of ethical perception has its historical origins in Aristotle's account of practical wisdom. In Book II of the *Nicomachean Ethics* (*NE*), Aristotle describes how finding the intermediate "mean" of each virtue between the vices of excess and deficiency does not depend on knowing a rule about how to act. Rather, it depends on "perception of the particulars."[1] He writes,

> In summary, then, if we do these things we shall best be able to reach the intermediate condition. But no doubt this is hard, especially in particular cases, since it is not easy to define the way we should be angry, with whom, about what, for how long; for sometimes, indeed, we ourselves praise deficient people and call them mild, and sometimes praise quarrelsome people and call them manly … But how far and how much we must deviate to be blamed is not easy to define in an account; *for nothing perceptible is easily defined, and since these circumstances of virtuous and vicious action are particulars, the judgment about them depends on perception.* (*NE* 1109b12–25)

On various readings of Aristotle, ethical perception is: "prior to moral judgment" and what a moral agent needs in order to identify a situation as moral in the first place (Blum 1994, 42); a kind of "discernment" or "faculty of discrimination" involving an agent's responsiveness to the ethically salient features of a concrete situation (Nussbaum 1990, 55); or an "aspect" of practical reason that enables a moral agent to discriminate what is relevant to ethical action and assessment (Sherman 1989). The exact relation between ethical perception and practical wisdom is a complex issue, especially so because practical wisdom is thought by Aristotle to be necessary for moral virtue. This is why Sherman says that, "*reading the circumstances* is informed by ethical considerations expressive of the agent's virtue" (p. 29). For the present purposes, we might just say in a provisional way that ethical perception is intimately connected to practical wisdom since one uses this kind of perception to grasp particulars (as opposed to universal principles), and the grasp of concrete particulars is necessary for a person to have practical wisdom as well as moral virtue.[2] What I suggest is that developing the skill to see what matters ethically can be learned independently of these linkages to practical wisdom and the development of moral virtue. If it should turn out that cultivating this kind of awareness about certain aspects of the world contributes to becoming morally virtuous in the Aristotelian sense, then this is even better. But my project is less grandiose because it does not aim for, or depend for its success on, the reader's achieving practical wisdom or moral virtue. As I describe in Chapter 2, acquiring ethical perception is like acquiring a general skill; one can develop the skill to *see* what matters ethically by learning how to pay attention to the right features of the world. Developing accurate ethical perception has value for each of us whether or not it leads to morally right action. I follow Blum (1994, 43) in his claim that being sensitive to issues of indignity and injustice, for example, is the setting for action. But doing the right thing does not capture the entirety of the moral dimension of ethical perception. Seeing these ethically salient features of the world has value in its own right.

From Aristotle (and others) I borrow the idea that ethical expertise is gradually acquired in degrees, and that this developmental process is experiential. The Aristotelian recommendation for how to develop moral virtue is by habituation, or by practicing how to understand, feel, and act in morally appropriate ways. This process of habituation of moral character has an experiential aspect.

> Young people can become mathematicians and geometers and wise in things of that sort; but they do not appear to become people of practical wisdom. The reason is that practical wisdom is of the particular, which becomes graspable through experience, but a young person is not experienced. For a quantity of time is required for experience. (*NE* 1142a12–16)

Aristotle is not so explicit about what kinds of experiences will function to cultivate practical wisdom and the ability to *see* what matters ethically, though he does emphasize that these experiences be "of the particular." I suggest here that narratives and stories can indeed profile the particular, and when they do so they may serve the same kind of educative function to develop in the reader or viewer a sensitivity to what is ethically salient about what is described or shown by the narrative. But more can be said initially to characterize the kind of expertise we are trying to foster by reading, watching, and thinking about narratives and stories.

Blum (1994, 46) suggests that to say about a person that "she is [generally] sensitive to particulars" is misleading. This is so because it implies that developing ethical perception is like developing a unitary faculty that will serve the moral agent equally well in all circumstances and with respect to many different kinds of particular situations.[3] However, when we survey the varying kinds of obstacles to seeing well that moral agents may have to overcome, we can understand how improving ethical perception involves cultivating not just one faculty of the agent but a variety of psychological abilities. Blum notes that some people may demonstrate more or less sensitivity to some kinds of situations rather than others. For example, one moral agent may be more sensitive to "suffering, racism, dishonesty, violations of someone's rights, [or] temptations to compromise one's moral integrity" (p. 46). Because the moral dimensions of these situations vary widely, it is plausible to suppose that learning to see these moral aspects of a situation is owed to a variety of psychological processes. Blum suggests that we explore *how* "imagination attention, empathy, critical reason, habit, exposure to new moral categories, and the like contribute to the formation of those [ethical] sensitivities" (p. 46). These general remarks are consistent with the methodology I follow here. Learning to see food justice is a domain specific skill. Focusing on the kinds of narratives that I recommend will ideally contribute to a moral agent's expertise in this area especially. I also agree with Blum that there are indeed a variety of ways to improve and develop ethical perception about food justice. This may include, as Blum suggests, practice, habit, and some forms of self-knowledge or therapy. But another contribution not mentioned by Blum that may help the agent to see well includes the experience of attending to narratives that wear the ethical dimensions of particular situations "on their sleeves."

Not just any kind of narrative will produce the right kind of sensitivity in a moral agent that is characteristic of ethical perception. Here I am thinking, in particular, about factual narratives, such as documentary films, biographies, autobiographical memoirs, or the genre of journalism called "narrative reporting." (I refer to these as "realistic narratives.") At their best these stories are written and presented in ways that engage us emotionally and inspire us to think critically. The reader or listener grasps the ethical content of the story by following the character or the narrator to an ethical conclusion. Specifically, I suggest that these stories should satisfy three particular conditions in order to facilitate learning to see what matters ethically.

First, the story should describe particular and concrete circumstances about individual people and their lives including their psychology, for example, why a person feels indignant, what she fears, or who she loves. As I will illustrate below sometimes this particularity makes reference to, and includes, geography of place. And sometimes this particularity can best be achieved by testimony from the inside when the narrator describes how things are *here*. The second demand on narratives is a truthfulness constraint having two parts; I call these *accuracy conditions.* One such accuracy condition involves the requirement that what is asserted in the story aligns with facts about the world. Another kind of accuracy condition involves construal. This sense of accuracy involves correctly classifying a particular set of circumstances under the right general moral concept, such as unfairness, honesty, or justice. The third condition on narratives is to position the reader or viewer to respond emotionally to the particular content presented or described. The right kind of story that cultivates ethical perception is one that emotionally engages the audience and invites us to cultivate appropriate feeling. What we need, of course, are examples to illustrate how ethical perception is conceptually designed to develop in the moral agent a sensitivity to what is ethically salient about *particular* circumstances, the sense in which ethical perception can and should be *accurate* perception, and the importance of cultivating and engaging the reader's *emotions* as a part of seeing well.

With the exception of Lawrence Blum's three abbreviated cases (discussed below), there is a surprising lack of real-world examples in the philosophical literature to guide us in understanding what ethical perception is. I begin with Blum's examples since one of my goals is not merely to summarize the already existing scholarship about this concept, but to actually articulate how an ordinary person might acquire ethical perception. So we should be prepared to consider examples of failing, as well as succeeding, to have ethical perception and to pair these examples with an explanation of *why* they are successes or failures. By seeing what obstacles confront moral agents in their attempts to achieve accurate ethical perception, we position ourselves to see what is ethically salient when we read a food justice narrative.

Particularity

Suppose I board an overloaded city bus and luckily find a seat just vacated.[4] At the next stop an elderly woman struggles up the steps with a bag of groceries in her arms. She wobbles unsteadily on her feet, and looks hopefully around for an empty seat but finds none available. I see her board the bus but I am distracted by work, still fuming about a meeting I attended with irascible members of my department. I do not *see* her predicament. And as a consequence I do not see how I can be helpful. I do nothing for her. However, another bus rider, Deb, notices the need of this particular person. She *sees* her frailty, her unsteady balance, and the ungainly package she is struggling to hold. By attending to these ethically salient particular details Deb "composes the scene in the right way," and performs an action that most of us would agree is the right thing to do in this situation. She stands and beckons for the elderly woman to take her own seat.

There are a few features of this example that are useful for constructing a fuller account of the concept of ethical perception. First, notice that my *failing* to see the ethically salient particulars in this setting can be explained in various ways. As described, I am distracted by recent events that I am mulling about angrily. (a) This may be a temporary lapse; or (b) it may be expressive of a more central characteristic of my moral character. Suppose reading (b) is true; I am self-absorbed and concerned with my own well-being more often than not. This way of describing things indicates a moral failing or a systematic flaw of my character. If I am characteristically distracted from others' needs, then my failure to see what is ethically salient in this case is attributable to my failure to be habituated in the direction of moral virtue.

What should we say about reading (a) of this example? This is the case where I am only temporarily distracted from what the elderly bus rider needs—a seat to rest her weary body. If this is a case of failing to have ethical perception, then am I morally culpable for this failure? Intuitively it seems not since *why* I fail to notice her need is not explicable by any deficiency of moral character. Blum considers this possibility when he remarks that if the [bus rider] fails to see what is ethically salient about the elderly passenger's need on a particular occasion then it might be "misleading" to morally criticize her since, "the failure may be too insignificant, and the moral relationship between the seated and standing passenger too attenuated, for it to count as a moral failure." However, it would so count if this were "expressive of a general failure to perceive discomfort" (Blum 1994, 33).

One essential feature of this example is the degree of seriousness of the situation perceived. If I do not notice a particular person's discomfort on a crowded bus, the failure may be, as Blum suggests, too insignificant to warrant moral criticism. But what if I fail to notice explicit verbal or physical abuse by another passenger directed at the frail, elderly woman with her hands full of packages? Let's assume that this is not merely a case where I do perceive the need of the elderly passenger, but I just do not know what to do about it. Nor is this a case where I perceive correctly, but I am fearful of intervening because a gang of mean-looking thugs are doing the harassing. Failing to see discomfort in this kind of case, even if it is temporary and on one occasion only, is more likely to be regarded as morally reprehensible due to the seriousness of what I fail to see. And the moral culpability of the perceiver may differ relative to the degree of seriousness of the object of perception even in the case where the failure to perceive what is ethically salient is not "expressive of a general failure to perceive discomfort," that is, attributable to a defect of moral character.

Interpreting the *Bus Rider* example as (b) points to a moral defect of character as a way of explaining my failure to notice what the elderly passenger needs. If, as Blum suggests, my failure to *see* is attributable to "attentional laziness" that is *typical* of me, then I should develop some practices to correct for that attention deficit as a general characteristic of my moral character. And what kinds of practices should this include? To answer this question we can look to Aristotle's remarks about the role that ethical perception plays in practical wisdom and how ethical perception facilitates the exercise of moral virtue. What counts as an obstacle to clearly seeing what is ethically salient may be characterized as a tendency in the direction of moral vice—being excessively self-absorbed, overly concerned with my own well-being, or tending in the direction of excessive temper as I continue to mull about the irascible colleague at the department meeting. Again, depending on exactly what psychology best explains my failure to see as a defect of moral character, the correction for this failure of perception will vary. For example, Aristotle explains the virtue of friendliness by recommending that we treat familiar companions as well as strangers, by "what is suitable for each," avoiding causing pain and sharing pleasure (*NE* 1126b25–35). At least part of this recommendation involves understanding what strangers or familiar companions need. So perhaps one way of correcting for the vice of being self-absorbed is to develop one's capacity and responsiveness to how others are faring—strangers included. The emphasis for correcting deficiencies of attention will still be on developing sensitivity to particular experiences. And this might well include, as Blum suggests, occasions for cultivating imagination, attention, empathy, critical reason, etc. (pp. 46–7). Consider, for example, how the following narrative about urban farming can focus our attention on the importance of particularity of place and testimony "from the inside."

In *Farm City: The Education of an Urban Farmer*, Novella Carpenter (Carpenter 2009) invites us to an unlikely farm setting—downtown Oakland. She begins in this way, "I have a farm on a dead-end street in the ghetto" (p. 3). A "squat-garden rebel" is what Ms. Carpenter calls herself as she gradually creates an urban farm on a garbage-strewn vacant lot adjacent to freeways, clusters of crack-heads, gangs of teenagers, and the homeless who gather at corner liquor stores. Here the author supplies us with the vivid particulars of place. But these initial descriptions do not create a sentimental love of that place—in either the author's eyes or from the reader's vantage point.

> As we cruised the neighborhood we took stock of our potential neighbors … The kids wore enormous white T-shirts and saggy pants; they counted their bills and stood in the middle of traffic, waving small plastic bags at prospective customers. Clearly a rough crowd … I was curious, and yet I had to admit it: they scared me. Could I really live here? Walk around the streets without worrying about getting mugged? (Carpenter 2009, 10)

The ethical argument of *Farm City* is just below the surface. Here we find values recommended about sharing food and the vital community life created by the activity of growing food and eating together. But in this case the community includes an unlikely cast of characters who eke out a subsistence living on the street. They do not buy Community Supported Agriculture shares of farm produce. They do not even work alongside Ms. Carpenter and her husband. But they are, nonetheless, beneficiaries of these activities. Sometimes they steal the just-ripe watermelons. Sometimes the food is offered to them for free. One is tempted to say that this story is only about Ms. Carpenter herself—a revisiting of her early childhood experiences lived with parents who practiced a self-sufficient lifestyle. But the author's questions about social justice flit in and out of the narrative. Who is this garden for? Why create a garden here? Gradually there emerges a more fundamental ethical rationale grounding this urban farming experiment. The particularities of place include individuals who are homeless, take drugs, and are unemployed. But we are introduced to them through the testimony of the narrator who reflects sympathetically about their needs. The more fundamental ethical issue is whether or not it is possible to bring about change for those who are living at the bottom rung of society.

In thinking about how the reader is guided to the ethical conclusion(s) of *Farm City*, Peter Goldie (2003) helpfully characterizes two points of view that narratives can display. The internal perspective is what we, as readers, identify with when we put ourselves in the position of the participant in a story. The reader is informed about what the narrator thinks and believes about his or her experiences, presented as a kind of "straightforward empirical report." However, the external perspective is the voice of the narrator who interprets and comments on events as he or she describes them. This perspective may be more evaluative and ethically complex, construing an event as unjust or an action as morally praiseworthy. These judgments may support the participant's reactions to events, or not. But at least in some cases the narrator attempts to move the reader to an ethical conclusion, using the narrator's experiences and first-person testimony from the inside as evidence in favor of this position.

While the narrative of *Farm City* begins by characterizing the activity of gardening as a personal lifestyle choice, there is clearly more at stake the longer Ms. Carpenter occupies this place and the more intimately her activities are integrated with the people living in downtown Oakland. The internal perspective of the narrator, together with her reflections on the particular unmet needs of her community, propels the reader toward a kind of activism. Urban farming begins to seem not only appropriate as a way of addressing food scarcity in the city, but also like something the reader can and should do oneself.[5]

Accuracy

Another example from Blum (1994, 36) is about Tim who is a white male trying to hail a taxi at a busy intersection. When a cab pulls up Tim is initially relieved to get a ride. Later, however, he reflects about the fact that the cab passed up a black woman and her daughter also standing on the curb. He *sees* the situation differently when he thinks more carefully about the circumstances. He comes to believe that the driver intentionally passed up the black woman and her daughter, and infers that he did so from racist motives; perhaps the driver prefers not to have blacks in his cab, or prefers not to drive to a neighborhood that he believes will be his destination if he picks her up.

Blum suggests that Tim's moral insight that he has witnessed a racial injustice involves two conceptually distinct cognitions. One is Tim's reflective *construal* of the situation. His awareness of the circumstances changes from relief about getting a cab, to noticing that the cabdriver passed by the black woman and her daughter. The second cognition is an *inference* that Tim makes about why the cabdriver failed to stop, attributing a racial motive to the driver. In doing so Tim employs the moral category of "racial injustice," using this to characterize what he has seen. Blum also adds that Tim's "take" on the situation is prior to any deliberation about what action, if any, to perform.

This example invites further discussion of two features of ethical perception. One is the relation between a person's awareness of particular details about a situation and the general moral category that captures her way of understanding these details. The second feature of the example worth exploring more carefully is the criterion for success of ethical perception. Tim's moral insight is presented as a case of seeing well. But if we are to recommend a way of cultivating ethical perception, then we should be prepared to say why and how this example qualifies as such.

Blum (1994) uses the term "perception" to include both Tim's construal that the cabdriver has passed up passengers, and his inference that this is a case of racism (p. 37). Tim's inference in this case relies on a general moral category, racism or racial injustice. By employing this concept Tim sees the cabdriver's actions in a particular way. Blum acknowledges that the cogency of the example depends on Tim already having this moral concept since if he failed to know what racism is he would be unprepared to classify the event as racist (though he may believe that passing up passengers in this way is still unfair). If ethical perception involves construing, knowing and applying moral concepts, and otherwise classifying particular events under some general moral category, then there should be some criteria for doing so correctly. The taxicab example raises questions about an agent's evidence and justification for construing a situation in one way rather than another, or subsuming a set of circumstances under a moral concept such as, racist, unfair, sexist, or unjust, etc. Blum remarks that it is unimportant whether or not Tim's "take" on the situation is correct as long as it is plausible. But this misses the point. If "accurate [ethical] perception is a good in its own right" (p. 34), then we should ensure that it is *accurate* perception rather than epistemically flawed perception that we are valuing. The taxicab example is incomplete in this respect since we are not privy to any evidence or confirming information that supports Tim's construal that the driver *intentionally* declined to pick up black passengers, or that this is a case correctly describable as racial injustice, the moral category Tim employs in his inference.

How best should we build accuracy conditions into a narrative about food? As we have seen, some ethical narratives, such as *Farm City*, supply the reader with an inside perspective on phenomena for ethical deliberation. In fact, some insights may be only accessed fully from the inside, where the narrator conveys her personal experiences not typically available to the reader. In McMillan's (2012) book, for example, we also get this inside interpretive perspective on what it is like to work in the garlic fields in the Central Valley of California, or to be a full-time worker at Walmart or Applebee's. These are experiences that may be foreign or unfamiliar to some readers so taking up this point of view may be crucially important.

Nonetheless, there are disadvantages to using autobiographical narratives as data for ethical deliberation. One difficulty is the challenge to objectivity that such personal reports create. Narrators may selectively choose what to include in their reporting, misremember events, embellish and exaggerate their experiences, or distort facts, either intentionally to elicit a sympathetic response, or unintentionally. This potential to stray from the objective does not disqualify narratives for ethical deliberation. It just means that we must apply to these some critical evaluation of the subjective content. Cheryl Misak (2008) argues for such a view in her article, "Experience, Narrative, and Ethical Deliberation," describing the external and evaluative perspective in narratives as "reason structured" and sensitive to critical evaluation. We need not merely accept the ethical conclusion as described by the narrator. Readers may assess this for "internal coherence, consistency with other evidence, simplicity, explanatory power, and so on" (p. 630).[6]

I concur with this approach as well as Misak's (2008) classification of narratives as "open to rational criticism" (p. 627). For example, the explicit ethical conclusion of McMillan (2012) is the need to make nutritious food available to everyone because there is inequality in our access to good food. The way in which this argument about inequality is made hinges on the particular details of McMillan's experiences, that is, from the inside point of view. But the general ethical conclusion about unequal access to nutritious food is supported by relevant facts and data. When McMillan finds herself gratefully accepting living conditions that most of us would describe as squalor, she cites statistics about living conditions for most migrant workers employed in the Central Valley of California. When she suffers from heat-induced injury working in the fields, she is ready to tell us about the general statistics of work-related injuries experienced by farmworkers, and the few options available to them. When she laments how difficult it is to pay rent, food, and living expenses from her job at Walmart or at Applebee's, she surrounds this lament with general information about pay and benefits by gender and race of those who work in the kinds of jobs where she herself is temporarily employed. So while McMillan is testifying to workplace conditions and lack of food choices, she is also bolstering the case that her own experiences are not idiosyncratic or anomalous. The documentation and referencing here is extensive. We might easily read this book for its academic compilation of data about workplace conditions, globalization of food, market conditions, labor rights, and immigration law. When McMillan narrates a new way of looking at the world based on her own particular experiences she moves the reader in this direction as well. The well-documented evidence for her ethical conclusion(s) support McMillan's moral insights and normative responses to events. So in this case we have more clearly satisfied what Misak would say is the critical review (or accuracy) of an internal narrative perspective.[7]

Emotional engagement

Another of Blum's (1994, 34–6) examples involves Theresa, a workplace administrator. Theresa's professional responsibilities include making accommodations for an employee, Julio, who suffers from a debilitating and painful condition in his leg. While Theresa fulfills her company's legal obligation to accommodate Julio, she does for Julio "less than what he needs and is entitled to." By Blum's description Theresa makes Julio feel uncomfortable bringing his concerns to her by putting him off, and giving him the impression that she believes he is too self-pitying. What she fails to see or grasp about Julio's plight is what having this condition means for him and the impact that his pain has on him. Part of the explanation Blum supplies for why Theresa does less for Julio than she should is that Theresa has a resistance to acknowledging pain in others, regarding this as a kind of weakness. She only feels contempt for people like Julio who suffer from painful conditions.

Blum classifies Theresa's failure to have ethical perception as a deficiency of character, and suggests that what she needs to correct for this deficiency is a better understanding of herself. Self-knowledge about why she regards pain in others (or in herself) as a weakness will go some way toward correcting her inability to see things from Julio's point of view. A closer examination of this example, however, reveals that adding self-knowledge to Theresa's moral repertoire might well be insufficient to correct her moral deficiency. Imagine that she does come to understand what prompts her reaction to pain as experienced by others (or herself). Suppose this resistance is attributable to a parent who mocked her reactions to scraped knees and toothaches as weaknesses. Theresa has managed to create a stoic persona in the face of pain as a result of these childhood experiences. Consequently, she now knows that she is reacting to Julio's painful condition because of her childhood-learned behavior. Nonetheless, knowing this information, in itself, will not create the kind of *seeing* that is responsive to Julio.

Even if Theresa takes steps to understand why she has developed an aversion to painful behavior in others, Theresa will still need to cultivate her affective responsiveness to individuals in order to complete her picture of what Julio needs in this case. There are two parts to this kind of responsiveness. In the first place, Theresa must hone her empathetic understanding of Julio and his predicament which will allow her to see things from his point of view. Second, Theresa's understanding of what Julio needs should include an appropriate emotional response to him, maybe compassion or sympathy. Empathy without this compassionate element may create understanding but not necessarily a concern for Julio himself. Blum (1994, 175) characterizes compassion by saying,

> Compassion is not a simple feeling-state but a complex emotional attitude toward another, characteristically involving imaginative dwelling on the condition of the other person, as active regard for his good, a view of him as a fellow human being, and emotional responses of a certain degree of intensity.

Other philosophers have also included this affective component in what it means to see what matters ethically. Nancy Sherman (1989) describes the affective component of ethical perception as central to the Aristotelian task of developing practical wisdom. What we learn from experience is a depth of understanding that emerges from someone who has "*lived through* the different moments of life, who has witnessed and judged not abstractly and at a safe distance (Aristotle *NE* 1142a12–16), but up close, where the face and look of others can have an impact on how one reacts" (Sherman 1989, 48). The person of practical wisdom has this experience to draw on that shapes not only their judgments about how to respond but also appropriate emotional responsiveness. When Aristotle recommends finding the mean for each virtue between the vices of excess and deficiency, he includes displaying the appropriate degree of emotional sensitivity in this general recommendation as well (*NE* 1109a23) (Sherman 1989, 49).[8] So we might say that one way of correcting for a deficiency of emotional engagement is to develop a sensitivity to features of living that include emotional attachments to projects, individual people, and moral ideals.

But there is not just one answer about what to do in order to engage the emotions to see with clarity what is ethically salient. For example, Nussbaum recommends allowing the novelist (or the artist) to guide us, as readers, to notice what is significant and important about how to live a good life. Literature can play this role of engaging our imagination and emotions by depicting complex characters living complex lives—their plights, suffering, desires, and loves.

> Moral knowledge, James suggests, is not simply intellectual grasp of propositions; it is not even simply intellectual grasp of particular facts; it is perception. It is seeing a complex, concrete reality in a highly lucid and richly responsive way; it is taking in what is there, with imagination and feeling. To know Maggie is to see and feel her separateness, her felicity; to recognize all this is to miss least of all. If he had grasped the same general facts without these responses and these images, in all their specificity, he would not really have known her. (Nussbaum 1990, 152)

A realistic narrative (or novel) can illustrate details of place and ways of living for particular people in such a way that makes possible the reader's cultivation of affective responsiveness to individuals and their plights. Jenefer Robinson (2005) calls this a "sentimental education" of the reader whose emotions are guided by a focus of attention on certain aspects of situations and characters. This process of education may happen when the narrative shows:

(1) The characters' focus of attention;
(2) Their thoughts about a point of view or the situation on which they are focused;
(3) How this point of view and focus of attention reflect the characters' desires, interests, and values; and
(4) The affective appraisals they make. (Robinson 2005, 158)[9]

These aspects of a story direct the reader or viewer of the narrative to attend to features of the characters' lives and situations that matter from their point of view. By attending to these ethically salient details the reader is guided to think and feel along with the characters. So when our own emotions are aroused by moral indignation or compassion about the plight of characters in the narrative, our emotional responses shape and inform our desires, values and beliefs about what we see or read. To illustrate how our emotional responses can be educated by a narrative, consider the documentary film titled *The Garden* (Kennedy 2008).

The Garden opens with a majestic aerial view of the largest urban garden in the United States—fourteen acres of green space in the middle of South Central Los Angeles. Partnering with the Regional Food Bank, the city offered this abandoned land to the neighborhood in 1994 as part of a larger set of initiatives to address food insecurity in a low-income Latino population.[10] Eventually 340 families established plots in the garden, growing food and plants native to their country of origin. These details are lovingly portrayed in our introduction to the South Central Farm. We meet the farmers themselves who give us guided tours, proudly pointing to and touching fruit and vegetables as they wander through the lush landscape. Children are frequently seen running through the garden or working the plots with their families. The film begins in this way by depicting a community of people who are invested emotionally with the activity of growing food and connected to one another in a place that functions also as a vibrant social center. The drama of the South Central Garden begins to unfold in 2004 when a notice to vacate the property appears on the chain link fence surrounding the garden. By organizing themselves and enlisting the help of civil rights lawyer, Dan Steamer, a temporary injunction is granted just two days prior to eviction.

But eventually this ruling is overruled on appeal, and the countdown to vacate the garden begins again. This time when the South Central Farmers regroup they take their cause to the public. Famous musicians and movie stars flock to the farm to fundraise. Sympathetic politicians are filmed receiving food from the farmers, and reporters interview the farmers and their supporters. Fundraising efforts target the 16.3 million asking price of the landowner, Ralph Horowitz.[11] But with seven days to eviction only $490,000 is raised. In an amazing turn of events, just two days before the farmers are evicted, the Trust for Public Land funded by the Annenberg Foundation steps in to donate $16 million dollars to purchase the land. Horowitz refuses to sell. On June 13, 2006, police in riot gear face off with crowds of supporters who are chanting and blocking access to the garden. The scene is chaotic with police pushing and dragging farmers and screaming supporters out of the way. Bulldozers eventually crash through the fence and crush the garden plots and plantings over the entire fourteen acres. These are the facts. But there are no words for how heartbreaking this story is to watch. Of course, the visual imagery is startling—the juxtaposition of the garden in full bloom at the beginning of the film with its graphic destruction at the end. But what also moves us sympathetically is hearing the farmers themselves say what the farm means to them. For many of the South Central Farmers political activism is new. The South Central Farm organizers, Rufina and Teza, encourage their co-workers to have courage to appear publicly and make their case at a City Council meeting. "The government is made by us," says Rufina. Their collective appeals to save the farm are sometimes in Spanish to mostly Anglo local politicians. By listening for the language of ethical values in this film we notice comments such as these: "It's because we are Latino that they are throwing us out, like animals" and "Something isn't right, not this time." After the temporary injunction is granted, one of the farmers declares, "This is the first step to finding justice." And "We will all be made equal under the law." But at the end of the film after the farm has been destroyed we hear this lament in halting English, "The last words in the Pledge of Allegiance say, 'Justice for All.' Where is the justice for poor people?" The viewer is positioned alongside the characters, seeing these events from their point of view. This response does not consist merely in the cognition that the South Central Farmers have been treated unfairly. It is more like the "hot feel" of moral indignation about their plight. And, our understanding of this injustice opens out to the treatment of poor people everywhere who are marginalized and politically powerless.

If we are looking for a rival ethical position here it is present but not particularly compelling. Ralph Horowitz says at one point, "It's my land;

this is my right [to develop the property]." Later, we hear only his voice in an interview over the phone. "They could have raised $100 million and I still wouldn't have sold the property. It's not about the money. I don't like their cause, and I don't like their conduct. What they should have said is, 'This is a gracious country. Thank you for letting me have this garden here. Thank you. Thank you.' "

One of the salient features of this particular narrative is that it invites us to look at the value of the South Central Farm from the inside. This is the point of view of those who are emotionally invested in the contribution that the garden makes to a particular community at a particular time. This emotionally engaged internal perspective on events is crucial for seeing how to "compose the scene in the right way." What we learn from a film such as *The Garden* is a depth of understanding and feeling that emerges for someone who has "lived through the different moments of life, who has witnessed and judged not abstractly and at a safe distance, but up close, where the face and look of others can have an impact on how one reacts" (Sherman 1989, 48). The person who seeks to undertake a "sentimental education" can use this narrative experience to shape not only how to feel but her ethical judgments as well.

Still we might be worried that the film manipulates us emotionally by presenting an uneven or biased depiction of the South Central Farmers and what they struggled to achieve. In order to answer this concern (in this case and for any narrative with ethical content) we ought to pair this story with the relevant context and factual background. According to Winne (2008), research on the inner city food system conducted by a team of UCLA graduate students in 1993 and led by faculty member Robert Gottlieb, produced a 400-page report titled "Seeds of Change." What they found in this part of Los Angeles was a wide gap in access to nutritious food between affluent and poor, and also a link between food insecurity and civil disturbances. Furthermore, there were documented substantial levels of hunger and food insecurity, cutbacks in government food programs that overwhelmed the emergency food system, few supermarkets remained in the inner city, and farmers' markets were not serving low-income populations. This additional information does not settle the issue about whether or not individual property rights should always prevail over the social goods created by urban farms. But it is harder to make such an argument in favor of Horowitz's right to develop his own property in this particular case once we know something more about the circumstances that impacted the lives of those who fought to keep the farm open.[12] Watching the unsuccessful struggle of the South Central Farmers guides us emotionally to the ethical conclusion that in this case the value of this particular farm to the community trumps Horowitz's right to sell and develop his property.

We might describe this kind of emotional education as "getting the tip." Nussbaum (1990, 160) says,

> Progress comes not from the teaching of an abstract law but by leading the friend, or child, or loved one—by a word, by a story, by an image—to see some new aspect of the concrete case at hand, to see it as this or that. Giving a "tip" is to give a gentle hint about how one might see. The "tip," here, is given not in words at all but in a sudden show of feeling. It is concrete, and it prompts the recognition of the concrete.

Learning to see food justice is facilitated by a narrative that educates the emotions of the reader or viewer. This kind of narrative reveals to us the concrete details of living, and the faces of individual people together with their desires, hopes, fears, or disappointments, who seek to overcome injustices in the attempt to nourish themselves.

Conclusion

Let's return to our start position. When Aristotle says that "perception [of the particulars] is understanding" and that older or prudent people who have acquired practical wisdom "see correctly because experience has given them their eye," he is emphasizing the way in which the acquisition of virtue shapes how the moral agent sees what matters ethically (*NE* 1142a12–16). But surely we can advise the ethical novice beyond the general recommendation to develop one's moral character through experience and habituation. The advice I would offer is merely one way of getting started by "giving a tip—a gentle hint about how one might [learn to] see." The tip for learning how to see what matters ethically in the domain of food justice involves reading narratives as descriptions of the particular lived experiences of those who attempt to nourish themselves.

Developing ethical perception is facilitated by what is seen or grasped—by attending to three features of a food justice narrative: particularity, accuracy, and emotional responsiveness. Particularity reveals what things look like from the inside. The narrator's point of view in the first person tells us something about how this person attempts to live and nourish herself. The accuracy of the narrator's testimony positions the reader or viewer to check the narrator's normative judgments and ethical conclusions against the facts relevant to the story, and the way these facts are construed or classified under more general moral concepts. And ideally such narratives elicit sympathetic responses to individuals and their plights. By emotionally educating the audience such stories may facilitate an understanding about what matters ethically. Novella Carpenter is the "squat garden rebel" who "creates a farm on a dead end street in the ghetto" of downtown Oakland. She directs our attention to what it is like to live in a place where the nearest "food" is sold in liquor stores. Tracie McMillan reminds us that manual labor, hard and underpaid, severely compromises a commitment to eating well. Perhaps the lesson of the South Central Farm is that even in cases where a community of people has an organized commitment to growing and eating their own food, the politics of place may nonetheless prevail to thwart this activity. What we should also notice about these particular examples is what they have in common. The residents of West Oakland, farmworkers in the Central Valley of California, and the South Central Farmers in South Central Los Angeles are constrained in their efforts to eat nutritional food because they are invisible, poor, or lacking political empowerment. The details of this marginalization are complicated by these groups' respective histories, geography, and social and political status. So more complete versions of these narratives will include the relevant background information as a way of getting the facts right. By identifying what features these stories share we become alert to structural inequalities that deprive individuals of the opportunity to be adequately nourished.

"Everyone wants good food," McMillan discovers. But choosing to eat nutritious food is, perhaps, not so easy to do, especially for people in particular sets of circumstances. McMillan (2012, 335) concludes her journey by saying,

> Fresh food, like water, is a shared and precious resource. Realizing this, for me, was akin to changing the focus on a camera. Adjust the lens in one direction, and only the meal on the plate will be clear. Adjust the lens again, and you can make out the contours of agriculture, with the rest a blur behind it. But make a final adjustment, so that the whole picture is sharp, and suddenly it becomes clear that our food is determined by far more than meals and fields. It's worthwhile, of course, to talk about food as a meal or as the product of a farm, but to engage with our meals solely on those terms is to ignore food's core essence. Food is not a luxury lifestyle product. It is a social good.

If food is a social good, then we should ask how to make nutritious food available to all people irrespective of their social and political location. Learning to *act* on behalf of food justice requires that we first "adjust the lens." It sounds pretty easy if we are talking about photography equipment; just rotate the focus dial on the lens of the camera until the image is sharp and clearly delineated. But acquiring clarity in ethical perception requires some additional skills. The ethical novice can develop *epistemic skills* to read food justice narratives for the subtle and complex features depicted in these stories. This is similar to the way that a stand-up comic can learn how to read his audience. Hint: He does not use a rulebook.

Garden Journal: Growing Seeds

The fluorescent lights we use in our living room to start our seeds are homemade. Chuck hammered together a pine frame with two supporting legs, about three feet high. The fluorescent tubes are suspended from an assembly of hooks and chains, designed to allow us to raise and lower the lights depending on the height of our new seedlings. Looking at these two contraptions this year Chuck decided that they were too high. Are we really growing seedlings into full-grown plants before we take them outside? Well, the rhetorical answer is "no" but, in fact, the peppers grew exactly that high before the weather permitted their transfer to the cold frame. Our garden mentor, John, threatened dire consequences if we moved our peppers outside too early. "Don't do it," he instructed us sternly. "You will get lots of plant growth but no fruit will set." How does he know these things? We usually do defer to John because he has been growing remarkable gardens for about forty-five consecutive years. But in this case what impressed us more than John's experience is that he described exactly our problem with peppers the previous year; tall spindly plants, but only a smattering of peppers late in the summer. So we raised the lights to accommodate the growing peppers in the house, which were more like trees by the time we placed them in the cold frame, the intermediary lodging for young plants on their way to the real outside deep beds.

Growing a garden together, as a couple, requires a division of labor. Luckily, I think Chuck and I have worked this out with only a few periods of quiet mutterings, "Why aren't you helping me here?" Or, "Why do I always have to do x?" where x is pull the weeds, water, harvest, mulch, etc. Chuck excels at many particular activities—garden related and otherwise. But one thing that I am particularly grateful for is his seed planting ability and zeal for this early spring task. By consulting a schedule of planting order (devised by John, of course), Chuck will get our potting soil into the small plastic containers, and choose the first seeds that will be started inside. Broccoli, cabbage, kale, peppers, and tomatoes will join us indoors in the living room for a few weeks. Then as we roll through the spring

I remember my responsibilities. The only two kinds of plants that I am in charge of starting are cucumbers and basil. Every year I plant too many. Sometimes this results in more pesto than we can eat in twelve months, or dropping off entire plants to the philosophy and foreign language departments, or chasing a neighbor down the street with a four-foot plant in late September before a frost warning. This year before all those small seedlings found a home in our garden, I arranged a plant seedling give away to members of the Broad's Book Club (a collection of girls who eat, drink, and sometimes even read a book for our book club meetings). May was the perfect month for me to get rid of these seedlings. Since our book club choice was Michael Pollan's (1991) Second Nature: A Gardener's Education, *the plant give away, reading assignment, and the early spring lettuce for the salad, were all part of an accidental theme for the evening.*

I have one more thing to say about Chuck's planting expertise. He knows how to handle small seeds. This is something which really sets him apart from other gardeners, I think. His hands, of course, are bigger than mine. But somehow he has more dexterity and "touch." No doubt this is connected to his ability to tie infinitesimal flies for fishing. Whatever it is, he can place tiny specks of plant particles into the earth, even counting the right number per square yard. The only seeds I can really plant are the large ones. Cucumbers and squash are best for me. Sunflower seeds I can handle as well. But I am no longer allowed to actually plant these because we have so many volunteering where they are not needed. That is another chapter in the story about how we divide the labor of gardening in our household.

2

Developing Narrative Skill

So far I have urged the reader to focus attention on particular features of stories about food, suggesting that we can learn something new about food justice in this way. Specifically, food justice narratives are counterstories that resist false or misrepresentative master narratives. And they do so by satisfying three conditions: particularity, accuracy, and emotional engagement. But I have not yet explained the methodology that underlies this kind of moral education. In this chapter I propose that learning to *see* food justice is part of a more general strategy for acquiring ethical expertise. Let's begin by supposing that the *ethical novice* is anyone who is in the beginning stages of developing ethical expertise. This includes young children but also adolescents, and even adults like you and me. As I suggest, classifying someone as an ethical novice has more to do with possessing an ability to cultivate certain skills rather than being a certain age. Still I profile the moral education of children in this chapter because I value the contribution made to this topic by practitioners of philosophy for children (P4C). What many who do this work recognize is that the philosophical novel is an ideal vehicle for fostering the skill of moral discernment to "read the situation." This skill is not necessarily enhanced by using rules or principles even at the beginning when the ethical novice is attempting to start the process of developing ethical expertise. Arnold Lobel's delightful story, "The Hippopotamus at Dinner," illustrates the role of the philosophical novel in facilitating those epistemic skills necessary for ethical expertise. This methodology is preliminary for understanding how food justice narratives contribute to ethical expertise in the domain of food justice. But first back to basics.

A common pedagogical strategy used in the moral education of children is to teach the ethical rule or principle. This is perhaps so ordinary as to be unremarkable. "Respect your elders," "Never lie," "Be kind to animals" are the kinds of rules that are easy to recommend (and post on bulletin boards). They span behaviors as well as dispositions or traits of character, for example, "Be a kind person." So rules can also be used to satisfy the demand articulated by some state mandated character education programs to expressly cultivate moral character in each grade level.[1] Nonetheless, most of us believe that moral education is more than just learning how to follow ethical rules or principles, no matter how initially plausible these rules may be. This leads me to ask a few questions about how best to cultivate ethical expertise. Are the teachers of rules right about using rules for young children but not for more skillful ethical reasoners? If so, how does the pedagogy proceed from rule-following to a more nuanced appreciation of ethical thinking, saying, and doing? Or perhaps the rule-following strategy is wrong from the beginning.

One very plausible answer to these questions is supplied by philosophers who are sympathetic to virtue theories of morality and, additionally, believe that virtues (and ethical competence) are acquired in much the same way that practical skills are acquired. Despite differences in the existing literature I refer to these as one kind of theory, "virtue as skills," since they all cluster around the idea that developing virtues and ethical competence is fundamentally like developing practical skills. Proponents of virtue as skills devote a fair amount of space to explaining what a skillful practice is, and what examples best illustrate skills versus non-skills. There is some uniformity here in that many of these accounts crucially depend on what is called the "Dreyfus model of skills," a five-stage theory of skill acquisition from novice to expert described by Dreyfus and Dreyfus (1991, 2004). For example, Stichter (2007, 2011) relies on the Dreyfus model to characterize the ethical expert as someone who does not rely on principles or theories to ground their expertise. In a more recent publication, Stichter (2011) focuses on how the ethical novice develops skillfulness, using the Dreyfus model to depict how virtue is initially acquired. Bloomfield (2001) cites and uses the Dreyfus model to defend a Socratic account of skills, or techné, in his explanation of practical wisdom. List (2013) follows Bloomfield (2000) in his exposition of practical wisdom and the concept of "diagnosis," citing the Dreyfus model of skill acquisition in turn. And the Dreyfus model is also employed by Jacobson (2005) who uses this account to characterize the ethical expert as one who does not require propositional knowledge to act correctly.[2] The examples employed to illustrate skillful practices range widely. These include medicine, navigation, chess, driving, hunting, angling, and firefighting, among others.

I will discuss a number of problems with the Dreyfus' five-stage model of skill acquisition. First, this model implies that developing ethical expertise in the early stages is a matter of using rules and general principles as action-guiding, but no attempt is made to explore *how* various kinds of rules function as action-guiding. Second, the examples used in the Dreyfus model to illustrate how skills are developed comprise a rather narrow class of cases that are especially suited to rule-bound explanations of skill acquisition. We need to consider other examples of skillful practice in order to appreciate how the nature of skillfulness extrapolates to the ethical domain.

The virtue as skills position can benefit greatly from what some moral particularists have said about how moral rules function, and the priority of the particular over the general.[3] I argue that the best account of how to develop ethical expertise is to guide the student to *see* and grasp what is ethically salient about the concrete particulars of a situation. These recommendations inspired by moral particularism suggest an alternative to the Dreyfus model of skillful practice; one where ethical expertise is developed by cultivating specific kinds of *epistemic* skills applied to narratives which are context-specific.

The Dreyfus model of skill acquisition

Dreyfus and Dreyfus (2004) describe a phenomenological model of skill acquisition that purports to be true of our experiences at the "level of daily life spontaneous coping." The five-stage model describes how the expertise of drivers and chess players progresses through the following stages: novice, advanced beginner, competence, proficiency, and expert. The authors hope that this analysis of skills will shed some light on how ethical expertise is acquired. Briefly, the novice level is described this way,

> Normally, the instruction process begins with the instructor decomposing the task environment into context-free features that the beginner can recognize without benefit of experience. The beginner is then given rules for determining actions on the basis of these features, much like a computer following a program. (p. 251)

This stage is illustrated by the case of driving and chess playing. The novice driver first learns about "interpretation free features" of this activity, such as the speedometer as an indication of speed, and the shifting of gears specified by the speed of the engine. The novice chess player learns the way each piece can move on the board, the numerical value for each kind of piece, and perhaps the following rule as a playing strategy, "Always exchange if the total value of pieces captured exceeds the value of pieces lost" (Dreyfus and Dreyfus 2004, 251).

The advanced beginner will have some actual experience. This allows her to modify "context free" rules in order to accommodate new aspects of the activity she is trying to master. The "situational aspects" are included in "instructional maxims" that the advanced beginner uses. These maxims are described in terms of features of the experiences accumulated by the learner. In chess the new player may begin to recognize situational aspects of positions on the board, and will be instructed to follow a maxim that references these aspects such as, "Attack a weakened king's side" (Dreyfus and Dreyfus 2004, 252).[4]

What Dreyfus and Dreyfus believe is the most interesting extrapolation from this skill model to the ethical domain occurs at the level of expert. At this level the proficient performer has a sufficient amount of experience to make decisions about a wide range of cases, acting with "an immediate intuitive response to each situation." About this stage of expertise the authors say,

> It seems that beginners make judgments using strict rules and features but that with talent and a great deal of involved experience, the beginner develops into an expert who sees intuitively what to do without applying rules and making judgments at all … If the skill model we have proposed is correct, and if every day ethical comportment is a form of expertise, we should expect it to exhibit a developmental structure similar to that we have described above. (Dreyfus and Dreyfus 2004, 253–4)

I believe that whatever developmental structure acquiring ethical expertise displays it is not entirely owed to the skill model described by Dreyfus and Dreyfus. To see that this is so I will comment on what is missing from this model that makes it inappropriate for explaining how ethical expertise is acquired.

Rules

One serious omission from the Dreyfus model of skill acquisition is a critical analysis of how rules are action-guiding in the context of practical activities. This is especially important if we are interested in how best to proceed in order to cultivate ethical expertise. Should we attempt to formulate definitional rules about honesty and justice for the beginner to grasp? Should we attempt to work these up into "instructional maxims" that make reference to some aspect of a situation to teach the advanced beginner? These questions lie at the heart of ethics education and they are not uncontroversial. Many character education programs now being implemented in K–12 schools build a rule-structured approach into teaching moral character. Rules such as "Be Respectful," "Be Responsible," and "Be a Good Citizen" grace the bulletin boards of many elementary, middle, and high schools. As well, professional studies programs in colleges and universities (Nursing, Business, and Counseling) attempt to teach their young professionals ethical conduct by relying on a top-down, rule-governed approach by employing ethical codes of the profession to resolve ethical dilemmas. So we have to ask whether or not the role that rules and principles play initially in the acquisition of skills really gets it right for certain kinds of practical activities, and whether or not it is appropriate to generalize from these activities to the ethical domain.

Recall that on the Dreyfus model of skills the novice begins to acquire a skill by grasping rules that specify "context-free features" of the activity that can be learned independently of experience. Rules also operate in guiding the behavior of the advanced beginner and the competent learner. Even though these "maxims" become increasingly more complex (and consequently less useful) as the contexts of experience become more numerous and varied, the model relies on an uncritical assumption that skills, in general, are acquired initially by grasping rules and general principles, where these are eventually relinquished at the expert level. It is not surprising that the Dreyfus model is described this way based on the example of learning to play chess. After all, it is a game with fairly specific rules the beginner must know before getting started with the actual play. But we may draw a different conclusion about how rules function as action-guiding by looking at a wider variety of skills and how different kinds of rules function in the context of these practical activities.

For example, Garfield (2000) offers a helpful distinction between kinds of rules used by umpires in the game of Australian soccer: the goal rule and the mark rule. What determines a goal in this game are "clear, unambiguous criteria." The relevant property can be described as, "the ball's being last touched by the foot (including the leg below the knee) of an attacking player and passing strictly between the big sticks (or their vertical extensions)." The mark rule requires judgment on the part of the umpire since a player gets credit for a mark if the umpire rules that the player "controlled the ball after having caught it on the full at least ten meters from the point at which it was kicked, or that he would have controlled the ball were he not tackled or otherwise interfered with in the process of taking the mark." Judging that the player "controlled the ball" is determined by some counterfactual conditions that may vary from game to game or league to league.

Garfield's description of how different kinds of rules function in a particular practical activity is helpful for understanding the role of rules in the Dreyfus model of skill acquisition. Consider the game of chess and the context-free rules learned by the novice chess player. These rules include the value of the pieces, how the pieces move on the board, some standard opening moves, etc. Not surprisingly these defining rules of the game are more like the goal rule. A person new to the game could learn them completely by reading a book about chess, perhaps memorizing these before even beginning to play, and "without any experience of [their] instances" (Garfield 2000, 188). However, if rules and principles are employed in the moral domain they need not be formulated in terms of explicit criteria of application like the goal rule. Garfield reminds us about the Wittgensteinian point that some rules are more like signposts in their capacity to guide action. We know how to interpret these if and only if we share a "form of life" that includes "shared judgments about particular cases, and shared practices of interpretation, application and similarity judgment" (p. 193). In other words, the ethical novice may acquire her skills by grasping the particular features of a concrete situation, using general rules or principles as summaries of these instances rather than as context-free definitional rules.

This more precise description of how rules are action-guiding, and in what kinds of circumstances, may seem peripheral to the main point the authors are making. By way of explaining what is important about their findings in the ethical domain, Dreyfus and Dreyfus align themselves with an account of ethics that minimizes the role of rules and principles. Experts of chess and driving seem to proceed without explicitly using general principles as action-guiding. Similarly, ethical experts are described as those who do not engage in rule-guided behavior. Dreyfus and Dreyfus describe their methodology as a "phenomenological" approach using chess and driving as cases of "daily life spontaneous coping." But the examples that fit the five-stage model are narrow indeed. In the next section we will see how other kinds of practical activities that are grouped under the category of skills fail to obviously exhibit the progression of skillfulness described in the Dreyfus model.

Priority of the particulars

Dreyfus and Dreyfus align themselves with Aristotle when they characterize the expert practitioner as someone who acts intuitively and spontaneously to do what is appropriate. But what the authors neglect to explore are the various kinds of skillful activities that Aristotle himself discusses. It turns out that the Dreyfus skills model is not entirely representative of Aristotle's position in emphasizing the particular over the general. Consider, for example, what Aristotle says in the *Nicomachean Ethics* (*NE*) about the virtue of wit:

> Then should the person who jokes well be defined by his making remarks not unsuitable for a civilized person, or by his avoiding pain and even giving pleasure to the hearer? Perhaps, though, this [avoiding pain and giving pleasure] is indefinable, since different people find different things hateful or pleasant. (*NE* 1128a20–25)

Here Aristotle is describing what is involved in reaching the mean virtue of wit between the vice of excess—vulgar buffoonery, and the vice of deficiency—a person who is boorish and stiff. The buffoon is one who will "stop at nothing to raise a laugh," even when this causes injury and pain to the victim of the joke. The boor is the kind of person who "would never say anything themselves to raise a laugh, and even object when other people do it (*NE* 1128a5–10). The mean virtue of wit seems to be someone with "dexterity." It is this kind of person who makes appropriate judgments about his audience saying, "what suits the decent and civilized person" as well as what is suitable to the "slavish" person. We see by this description that the art of joke-telling cannot be captured entirely by a collection of general rules about how to tell jokes. Since "different people find different things hateful or pleasant," the joke teller must be sensitive to his audience of the moment and their sensibilities (*NE* 1128a25). These are the particulars that must be grasped if he is to make wise or excellent choices in this area.[5]

Furthermore, whatever rules or general principles are employed may function as summaries of particular choices made or as rules of thumb. The humorist might remind himself before he tells a joke, "Don't offend a civilized audience with a dirty joke." But he still needs to identify this audience as one to which the rule applies, that is, civilized, and classify a particular joke as "dirty" relative to this audience. Without this particular information about what he sees from one joke-telling opportunity to the next, the general rule will never get its grip on the appropriate context. Nussbaum (1990, 71–2) describes this point in the following way,

> Excellent choice cannot be captured in general rules, because it is a matter of fitting one's choice to the complex requirements of a concrete situation, taking all of its contextual features into account. A rule, like a manual of humor, would both do too little and too much: too little, because most of what really counts is in the response to the concrete; and this would be omitted. Too much, because the rule would imply that it was itself normative for response (as a joke manual

> would ask you to tailor your wit to the formulae it contains), and this would impinge too much on the flexibility of good practice.

Crucially, for understanding the difference between this interpretation of Aristotle and the Dreyfus model, the "manual of humor" will not serve the novice joke-teller any better than the expert. What the novice begins with is not a formula for telling jokes that can be learned independently from all actual instances of joke-telling. "Don't offend your audience" is action-guiding only because it depends for its interpretation on actual cases where offense is taken or not, depending on what jokes the humorist tells, the sensitivities of the audience, and so on. The imprecision of the rule here, and hence its inadequacy, is not explained by the sheer number of "situational aspects" the competent joke-teller faces, as Dreyfus and Dreyfus say about the competent chess player. Rather, it is by nature of the practical activity of joke-telling itself that it cannot be captured by universal definitions, but by attending to the relevant and particular features of the experience from the beginning.

According to Aristotle, the importance of the particular case is illustrated by other practical activities such as medicine and navigation. Consider the following passage:

> Let this be agreed on from the start, that every statement about matters of practice ought to be said in outline and not with precision, as we said in the beginning that statements should be demanded in a way appropriate to the matter at hand. And matters of practice and questions of what is advantageous never stand fixed any more that do matters of health. If the universal definition is like this, the definition concerning particulars is even more lacking in precision. For such cases do not fall under any science or under any precept, but the agents themselves must in each case look to what suits the occasion, as is also the case in medicine and navigation. (*NE* 1103b34–1104a10)

We might be struck by Aristotle's claim that in "matters of practice" (medicine and navigation) agents must look in each case to "what suits the occasion." With respect to navigation let us suppose that we have a navigation "textbook." For sailing this might include tide charts, depth of water in geographical locations (in bays or around rocks). But still the navigator must attend principally and primarily to the details of place. The practice of sailing from point A to B is complicated by the particularities of wind, sea, light, as well as the condition of the boat during a particular voyage. A wise sailor knows how to negotiate these conditions by attending to the particularities. In fact, he might not get to point B unless he sees and compensates for the force of the wind or the drift of the tide.

In other words, the textbook couched in terms of how things are generally will not be the primary or most important information that guides the navigator. Instead it is the sailor's attention to the particular details of traveling from A to B that result in excellent choice—a successful voyage.

When we focus explicitly on those examples of virtue (wit) and practical activities (medicine, navigation) discussed by Aristotle, we are bound to characterize the nature of skill differently than if we use the example of chess playing. First, acquiring skillfulness in joke-telling, medicine, and navigation does not begin by learning a formula or context-free rules. This description of skill acquisition is no truer for the novice than it is for the expert. What the expert has, of course, is more experience with particular cases. But even the novice navigator, for example, will be urged to attend to those features that are relevant to how the ship will sail today, in this weather, in these tides, in this particular boat, and so on. So, one important strand of Aristotle's position neglected in the Dreyfus model is that how an agent acquires virtue is by perception of individual cases, as opposed to grasping a formula, definition, or rule (*NE* 1142a23).

Second, even though Dreyfus and Dreyfus align themselves with Aristotle in characterizing their skill model as "empiricist," this model deviates from what some commentators have said about Aristotle's account of practical skills, practical wisdom, and virtue. D. S. Hutchinson (1988) describes the fourth-century debate about skills as a case of "Aristotle celebrating what Plato despaired of, that medicine, like helmsmanship, is an essentially imprecise knowledge" (p. 40). According to Hutchinson, one disagreement between Plato and Aristotle was about the nature of this imprecision. Plato believed that the science of medicine was comprised of a collection of profound truths; a theory or general account that was difficult to apply in practice because of the number of variables, though the theory itself was not imprecise (pp. 34–5). Aristotle, on the other hand, insists that medicine and virtue are domains where no precision is possible. Hence, skillfulness in practical activities is acquired by estimation, where this is a "necessary and natural part" of the activity (*NE* 1106b15–16, 1106b28). But in these cases the nature of estimation is not owed merely to the imprecision of applying a general rule or definition in various settings. As Hutchinson (1988, 43) says, "for Aristotle, the estimating comes in before the problems of application, which, in turn, add to the overall effect of imprecision."

This important difference between Plato and Aristotle about the nature of skills as well as virtue is not captured by the Dreyfus skill model since on this model rules or maxims will work fine for the advanced beginner and competent learner until the number of variables become too numerous (Dreyfus and Dreyfus

2004, 252). By this description rules are inadequate because they are difficult to apply as the practitioner faces new and varied conditions. But according to Hutchinson's interpretation of Aristotle, rules are inadequate because the domain of knowledge itself is imprecise in the areas of medicine, navigation, and virtue. By using few examples of practical activities (and especially chess) to characterize skills, Dreyfus and Dreyfus sacrifice this important feature of Aristotle's position and risk misrepresenting what it means to acquire skillfulness in the ethical domain as well.

The philosophical novel

The criticisms articulated in the last section suggest a way to improve the model of ethical skillfulness. In doing so we can make such an account consistent with cultivating exactly the narrative skills required to read stories about food justice. Suppose we try to explain how ethical expertise develops by attending not to practical activities like chess, but to those skills that we hope to cultivate in the ethical novice. This strategy differs from most of the virtue as skills literature because it *begins* with a characterization of ethical expertise, and then seeks to identify those skills that will contribute to developing just this kind of expertise. Let's start at the beginning by surveying how practitioners of P4C describe ethical inquiry and how, in particular, the philosophical novel contributes to learning these ethical skills.

Lipman et al. (1980) say that one aim of the P4C curriculum is to develop ethical understanding. And this means to develop in students "ethical sensitivity, care, and concern." The authors remark:

> The aim of ethical inquiry is not to teach children certain particular values; it is rather an open-ended, sustained consideration of the values, standards, and practices by which we live, discussed openly and publicly so as to take all points of view and all facts into account. It is the assumption of ethical inquiry that such discussion and reflection, taking place in an atmosphere of mutual trust, confidence, and impartiality, can do more to foster moral responsibility and moral intelligence in children than any system that merely acquaints them with "the rules" and then insists that they "do their duty." (p. 189)

Accordingly, we should replace the teaching of moral rules with something more pedagogically "messy." This includes using the philosophical novel as a vehicle to introduce the "complexity and ambiguity of moral situations" as they occur in the practical lived experience of the characters in the novel (Lipman et al. (1980, 176). What matters here is less like doing the right thing on a particular occasion, and more like creating a whole person who can claim to possess a kind of global integrity with respect to her values. These may be displayed in her consistently thinking, saying, and doing over a longer span of time. For example, in the philosophical novel *Lisa* intended for middle school age students, Lisa wrestles with her love for the taste of chicken and her awareness that she is eating an animal that is in some respects like her. Because Lisa does not approve of "killing birds and animals," she worries about a kind of inconsistency between her thoughts and actions.

What contribution does the philosophical novel make to developing ethical integrity in the whole person? According to Lipman et al. (1980, 176), the value-added feature from the novels is context. The novel is perfectly suited to illustrate the "multi-dimensionality of moral situations and choices … and the consequences of these choices" as the characters experience the ethical dimensions of their lives. Ethical concepts such as fair, right, or good, are not introduced in the novel by first defining these terms. Rather, the meanings of these concepts are explored as they occur in the concrete day-to-day events of the characters in the novel, as well as in the experiences of those children reading the novel (p. 190). Likewise, when rules and standards are discussed it is not by means of abstract principles that have an inviolable status. The plausibility of such rules and principles are examined in their application to practical living.

A nice example of this occurs in chapter 5 of the novel *Lisa* (Lipman 1983). When Harry asks his dad, "Is it ever right to lie?" he hopes to get a simple, "yes" or "no" answer. Harry is disappointed in this expectation. Instead his dad supplies him with some criteria for deciding whether or not a lie is wrong in a particular case. The story of the three-headed giant introduces some features of context that matter to this determination: (a) "whether the thing you say is true or false"; (b) "what you're trying to do by saying it"; and (c) "whether what you say is hurtful to anyone" (p. 37). Harry's dad qualifies these criteria by saying that if a person knows that an utterance meets all of these conditions, then "you [can] be pretty sure" it is morally wrong. If it meets only some of these three conditions, "you just have to guess." Probably this remark means to use some judgment depending on the circumstances. Later, Harry and his friends have a chance to apply these criteria to determine whether or not Mark has been inconsistent when he answers the same question differently on two different occasions. In the first case he lies about Maria's whereabouts to thugs who want to bother her. And then he tells the truth about where Maria can be found when asked by her friend, Millie (p. 39). The relevant difference between these two cases depends on the intentions of the inquirers, as well as with the harmful consequences that might ensue by Mark's truthfully revealing Maria's whereabouts to the thugs.

The most interesting aspect of this example for the study of ethical rules is that Harry qualifies his initial endorsement of the rule, "Never lie." This rule is defeasible, replaced by attention to the circumstances about particular cases. What the characters discover is that the situations of Mark's two utterances are not the same; "They [are] miles apart" (Lipman 1983, p. 39). What features contribute to the cultivation of ethical expertise in the philosophical novel are judgments about what counts as like or unlike particular situations. But what has happened to the ethical rules that we are so fond of articulating to children in ethics education? Have we given these up entirely to be replaced by judgments about particular cases of lying, for example? There is considerable disagreement among philosophers about the answer to this question. For the moral particularist, taking context seriously contributes to genuine skepticism about general rules and principles.[6] For example, McNaughton (1988) says,

> Moral particularism takes the view that moral principles are at best useless, and at worst a hindrance, in trying to find out which is the right action. What is required is the correct conception of the particular case in hand, with its unique set of properties. There is thus no substitute for a sensitive and detailed examination of each individual case.

The teacher or student of ethics need not enter into the metaphysical debate about whether or not the "shape" of the moral domain is constituted by general principles, or irreducible particular cases constituted by "unique set[s] of properties." But she may still benefit from the methodology suggested here, described as a "sensitive and detailed examination of each individual case."

Epistemic skills

We might do well to follow Little (2001a, 172) in her description of the methodology that can guide our examination of particular cases. She proposes a skill model of moral discernment.[7] Like any practical skill where we develop expertise such as, driving, parenting, or diagnosing disease, developing ethical expertise takes time. Understanding moral categories like cruelty or kindness is best described as latching onto paradigmatic instances of these when they are experienced in concrete circumstances.[8] Little remarks, "it takes experience and subtlety to understand the difference between being kind and being nice, between false and genuine charity, between tough love and abandonment" (p. 173). As competence is developed in recognizing the straightforward paradigmatic instances of moral concepts, we further learn "how to go on" by extending these paradigms to other more complex and varied contexts. In doing so we employ the epistemic skills of judging patterns of similarity and relevance between like cases of kindness, fidelity, or cruelty (p. 177).[9] However, according to Little, we are not merely left with judgments about particular cases. Ethical rules and principles still have a role to play as rules of thumb and as aids for the ethical novice. For example, an ethical novice may benefit from the rule, "Always tell the truth," as she struggles to gain competence with the concept of fidelity. But Little warns that we should not confuse the heuristic value of general rules and principles with their truthfulness.[10] Learning the rule itself is no substitute for learning and acquiring the skills of moral discernment.

> But the usefulness of such principles to novices does not mean reliance on them is the model for experts. With moral wisdom, as with any skill, it is a sign of maturity to be able to let go of the guidebooks, cookbooks, and primers, and to exercise directly one's ability to judge. (Little 2001a, 173)

The presumption that using general rules does have heuristic value for the ethical novice is rarely questioned.[11] Nor do we ever learn who counts as an ethical novice, much less how the skills of moral wisdom emerge from rule-following for one who acquires moral maturity. Maybe it goes something like this. Start with simple ethical rules, for example, "Always tell the truth." Add to these complicating features of context. Produce a person with moral discernment and moral wisdom who knows when to leave the rules behind.[12] I agree with the description of the end product but wonder about the first two steps. The description of the ethical expert as one who is "able to let go of guidebooks, cookbooks, and primers" does not guarantee that we are on the right track from the beginning. And, one might suspect that a novice cook who has been trained to follow the recipe will yield a mature cook who continues to follow recipes even in modified form. Unless the cook is guided by a specific recommendation to leave the recipes behind, why would she deviate from a workable methodology for cooking, especially if she routinely produces pretty good meals?

By describing ethical expertise as a collection of skills that require development and practice for their exercise to maturity, the answer is clear enough. Someone who is practicing to become an accomplished musician or an expert golfer should practice exactly those skills that comprise the activity she is trying to master.[13] For the musician this might be fingering, tone, and intonation. For the aspiring golfer this might include the components of the swing itself, and different strokes needed in conditions where the varieties of turf influence how to hit the ball. Even if we are instructed to "keep your head down" or "keep your eye on the ball," we are not tempted to confuse this recommendation with the skill itself that we are attempting to learn; the golf swing. But by using ethical rules as the start position for acquiring ethical expertise the temptation to misunderstand the skills one is attempting to learn is greater. Little is correct to say that when we emphasize principles as guides to ethical decision making, we are in danger of allowing "skills of discernment, interpretation, and judgment" to atrophy (Little 2001a, 179).

It seems to me that one way of guarding against this danger is to *begin* the process of moral education by introducing contextual circumstances into ethical thinking, saying, and doing, in all of its complexity. There is evidence of exactly this strategy in the P4C novel, *Nous*, intended for primary school students in grades 3–7 (Lipman 1996b). Here, for example, the ethical issue of lying is explored by examining the circumstances in which a statement might count as a lie, when and how we use the concept of fairness, and when (in what situations) someone can be said to advocate cruelty.[14] This approach to teaching moral concepts is by design. In the introduction to the teacher's manual that accompanies *Nous*, Lipman remarks,

> It would be a relatively simple matter for the child to construct a list of actions and to memorize which are approved and which are disapproved. Unfortunately, matters are not so simple. The signal they get from adults is not merely that "X is right, but Y is wrong." What they pick up, rather is that "X is right, except under circumstances a, b, c, d … n" And so children learn that values are contextual rather than free-standing. Nothing is good or bad, right or wrong, in independence: provision must always be made for the setting or surrounding in which it occurs. But while identification of the act may not be very difficult, it is far from easy to read the circumstances that make up the context of the act. (p. ii)

Recall one question I asked at the beginning. Are the teachers of rules right about using rules for young children but not for more skillful ethical reasoners? Perhaps not according to Lipman since even from an early age the philosophical novel, with its attention to context and its disavowal of ethical rules, has purchase.[15] What this suggests is that even for the ethical novice the rule-following pedagogy is wrong from the beginning. In order to see *how* the epistemic skill model of ethical expertise might be used in a narrative for children as well as adults, consider Lobel's (1980) delightful fable. We may treat the analysis of this fable as an opportunity to practice the epistemic skills required to read food justice narratives in later chapters.

"The Hippopotamus at Dinner"[16]

Hippo's eyes are bigger than his stomach, and his stomach is big indeed. When Hippo demands service at a restaurant, he wants it delivered fast, and he wants a lot. When the waiter returns with his plate Hippo is outraged. He insists that the portions he receives "would not satisfy a bird."

"I want a bathtub of bean soup, a bucket of Brussels sprouts, and a mountain of mashed potatoes."

Hippo eats the whole dinner, happy at last to have as much food as will fill his appetite. But when he prepares to leave the table, oops; he is stuck. His stomach is caught between the table and the chair. As time passes the other diners leave. Then the cooks put away their pots and the waiters hang up their aprons. Hippo sits forlornly by himself after everyone is gone. He admits, "Perhaps I should not have eaten quite so many Brussels sprouts." The moral of this sad story does not only apply to what we pile onto our dinner plates. Lobel writes, "Too much of anything often leaves one with a feeling of regret."

We might begin to cultivate the kinds of epistemic skills Little describes by paying attention first to the concrete details involving a particular Hippo "caught" in a tight situation. The story does not begin with a general rule or principle about how much to eat, though it ends with a fable moral that is couched in rather general language. The relevant features of this story identify appetite as the theme linking "too much" to "feelings of regret." But how we apply the fable moral to other kinds of cases requires judgments of similarity to this *privileged* case about Hippo and how much he eats (Little 2001b).[17] It remains for the reader of Lobel's fable to investigate whether or not the fable moral, "Too much of anything often leaves one with a feeling of regret," applies to other cases as variations on this theme. For example, when we spend too much money, are we left with a feeling of regret? This is not the same feeling, of course, that we have when we are stuck behind a table because we have eaten too much food. But there is, arguably, a variation on the theme of gluttony with respect to bodily appetite that is connected to financial overindulgence and, perhaps, an accompanying regret about overspending. Deciding how to characterize financial overspending depends on the particular case. The relevant features include how much one spends, the reasons for overspending, one's fiscal resources, and so on. Another possible variation of the fable moral theme about bodily appetite might concern whether or not overindulgence on behalf of others is like, or unlike, overindulgence on behalf of the agent who acts. Does too much charity, for example, leave one with a feeling of regret? Importantly, even though the fable about Hippo is a children's story it might also inspire moral experts to reflect more deeply about the conceptual terrain surrounding these ideas about what counts as too much and for whom, as well as how this is associated with feelings of regret.

In each attempt to apply the fable moral to cases beyond the privileged case involving bodily appetite what we need to employ are fine-grained and nuanced judgments about patterns of similarity to the privileged case. As Little (2001b, 39) remarks, "an integral aspect of knowing 'how to go on' is knowing what counts as, and having the skill to navigate, what is deviant and normal, paradigm and emendation, theme and variation." The story of Hippo and its accompanying fable moral illustrate how we employ epistemic skills of comparative judgments to move back and forth between the story particulars, and applications to new cases beyond the paradigmatic features of the story itself. In this way we focus explicitly on the skills of *seeing* the ethical particulars of a story in order to cultivate moral discernment.

Conclusion

From the philosophical novel we learn that "values are contextual rather than free standing" (Lipman 1996a). The result of pairing this practice and methodology with a skill model of ethical expertise has wide-ranging implications for moral education. As Lipman et al. (1980, 166) remark,

> The sensitive discrimination of similarities and dissimilarities among situations is of fundamental importance to the child's moral development. The child must be able to take into account a large number of subtle and complex features of situations—their metaphysical, aesthetic, and epistemological as well as their moral aspects—that are present whenever we compare or contrast such situations with one another.

As the authors realized, in order to notice the "subtle and complex features of situations" the student must develop the skill to "read the situation" since, without this ability "you have nothing" (Lipman et al. 1980, 193). The P4C curriculum (novels, dialogues, and teacher's manuals) all aim to develop this skillfulness of perception or judgment to notice the particular case, for example, this is a case of cruelty, or this is a case where the speaker's intention is malicious. In this sense the philosophical novel is a model for how we should teach ethics, regardless of age. But this methodology for developing ethical discernment described here extrapolates beyond the philosophical novel. We are now prepared to practice the epistemic skill to "read the situation" in stories about food justice.

Mother Hubbard's Cupboard: Food Pantry

My first shift at the MHC food pantry begins at 3:00 P.M. on a Tuesday afternoon in Bloomington, Indiana. Since there were no scheduled orientations for me to attend, Erin says she will let me shadow Alyssa in the refrigerated section for an hour, and then I can take over that spot for the second hour. Really, what it means to "shadow" in this setting is just to get in the way. The space is small; boxes and crates of cold or frozen products (soymilk, yogurt, tofu, meats, and ready-cooked meals) just unloaded from the truck and sitting in the aisles have to be stacked in the refrigerators or freezers. Some will go on the shelf for clients to choose from, other products will go into storage freezers or cold areas to be pulled out later. What goes where and how to decide is completely mysterious to me. There is some organizational method but I can only watch a bit helplessly as it is implemented. Finally, Alyssa takes pity on me and gives me some directions for stacking meat in storage freezers, and tells me when to put these on the shelves for clients.

Elsewhere in the pantry, dry goods (canned corn and beans, breads, and canned fruit) are being stocked on shelves, and the produce section is being organized. And what lovely produce indeed. Bins of kale, bok choy, winter squash, apples, and bananas line the shelves. Even in the second week of November the vegetables are still coming in from the community gardens run by the MHC, and they literally glow with vibrant, deep autumn colors—purples, dark greens, oranges, and yellows.

As we near 4:00 P.M. a line begins to form outside the front door of the MHC pantry. Before the clients are allowed to enter Erin announces that volunteers can shop for themselves. I am surprised to see almost all of these volunteers wandering throughout different sections of the pantry to help themselves to products they had just laboriously stored. I guess the reason why I am surprised is that first, I did not know volunteers were allowed to this. Second, it never occurred to me that they would need to do so. I assumed that volunteers in food pantries are financially secure, and that they donated their time for people who are not financially secure. The volunteers I am working with at the MHC are comprised of students, mothers with their children in attendance, single men, as well as those who are probably classified as "special needs." Alyssa, my trainer, is a graduate student at Indiana University working on her PhD dissertation. She has her eight-year-old son with her who is lugging a grocery bag filled with produce. When we got to talking Alyssa tells me she is headed off to a conference on the East Coast to give a paper presentation. How do we tell when someone is food-insecure?

At 4:00 P.M. the door opens for clients. They first stop is to sign their names on a dated register. You may shop once a week at the food pantry if you meet any of these guidelines (though there is no verification of this information required):

- *You cannot make ends meet to buy food*
- *You qualify for Supplemental Assistance Nutrition Program (SNAP) benefit*
- *You cannot work at this time because of an illness or injury*
- *You lost your job in the past month*
- *You are homeless*
- *You are over fifty-five years old*
- *Someone in your household is pregnant or nursing*
- *You are a single parent and have not received child support lately.*

Plastic bags are carefully folded by volunteers to give to the clients for shopping. Every item on the shelves has a limit per family or individual. Clients can take as many packages of dried plums as they want (because these are in abundance). Still the prunes are a hard "sell." And they may take as much bread as they want since this has a very short shelf life. The day I am working for some reason the bread supply is meager. We run out before the pantry closes at 6:00 P.M. Signs posted outside inform clients that meat is available at 5:00 P.M., and desserts will come out at 5:30. The staggering of goods on the shelves makes shopping possible for people who cannot be in line right at the opening bell.

Since I am working the refrigerated section of the pantry I need to keep track of the frozen meats and cold items, replacing these with goods from the storage areas when there are fewer items on the shelves. But I am told not to load up the shelves because this will be too tempting for shoppers to take more items than they are allowed. There is a lot of frozen chicken to put out, and this is mixed with sausage links, pork chops, chicken gizzards, and even some soup bones. At 5:30 I begin to load one side of the freezer with meals, and today it is boxes of Steak-Ums frozen sandwiches. These are popular. The tricky part of my job is to make sure that clients do not take more than they are allowed. One meat item is allowed per family, in addition to one Steak-Ums sandwich box. But some people are shopping for others by proxy, and the limits are different for larger families. So when I see two or three packages of meat go into the plastic bag of one shopper, I am not sure what to do. I say, hesitantly, "I think you are only allowed one meat." "Oh yea," he says. "But I'm trying to feed 8 people in my family." This sort of floors me. I just shrug and let him continue to shop. Who am I, the food pantry police? Later, I see a more egregious case of taking too much meat but another veteran volunteer is asking politely for some of the packages to go back on the shelf. So I do not need to do anything.

When the line of shoppers is snaking through the pantry, I see an acquaintance from the University, together with her husband and their two young children. I knew her husband was out of work but I did not know that this was part of the solution to keeping her family afloat. All of a sudden I realize that it might be embarrassing for her if we meet in this line, with me volunteering and her availing herself of the food. So I quickly back up behind a shelf while she chooses meat. Food insecurity is taking shape for me in a very concrete way—individual people with faces and names, in a variety of circumstances, and with particular stories to tell about why they need to stand in line at the MHC food pantry.

3

Food Insecurity: Hungry Women

Many hunger relief organizations and international development organizations use stories to profile individual people who are food-insecure. In this chapter I explore the meaning(s) of a representative class of such stories about who is hungry and why. These stories are designed to reveal the "faces" of hunger. As well the narratives shape our responses to hunger by implying what kinds of solutions are appropriate. The philosophical issues that emerge from stories about food insecurity are a complex tangle of moral concepts about accidental bad luck, personal responsibility, deservingness, and justice. For example, when we explain how a particular woman comes to be hungry by attributing to her misfortune or accidental bad luck, then we may not see how her plight is also a function of systemic injustices and broader failures of institutional inequities. In these cases we might come to believe falsely that food insecurity is explained largely by idiosyncratic conditions that are specific to individual people. Accordingly, we may not see that a solution to hunger requires political justice. What is worse is that some stories about who is hungry and why contribute to a damaging master narrative about food insecurity.

Recall that Nelson (2001, 6) describes master narratives as "stories found lying about in our culture that serve as summaries of socially shared understandings … often archetypal, consisting of stock plots and readily recognizable character types" that we use to make sense of our experiences and inform our moral intuitions. For example, Young (2011) writes that in the last two decades we have seen a shift in the discourse about those who are poor. This discourse implies that the causes of poverty and hunger depend on the characteristics and behavior of the poor themselves. One way of describing this "deviant" behavior is that those living on the margins of our society fail to exhibit a sufficient degree of personal responsibility for their lives. This purported failure of responsibility is used to explain how some, but not others, have become poor and dependent on social services.

Why does this matter? Nelson (2001) describes how identities can be damaged by master narratives, contributing to the oppression of individual people or the subgroups to which they belong. One of the ways oppressive master narratives can damage identities is by deprivation of opportunity when such a story imposes a degrading identity on a person or a group, characterizing them as morally subnormal or abnormal. When oppressive master narratives find their way into public policy debates about Supplemental Nutrition Assistance Program (SNAP) benefits, for example, what hangs in the balance is the very real possibility that those who are food-insecure may suffer a serious deprivation of opportunity to nourish themselves. For example, consider Representative Steven Fincher, a Republican congressman from Dyersburg, Tennessee, elected in 2010 by tea party constituents. Between 1999 and 2012, Fincher collected close to US$ 3.5 million in farm subsidies for corn and soybeans from the federal government. He recently voted for a farm bill that omitted SNAP benefits—a position he defended by stating, "The role of citizens, of Christianity, of humanity, is to take care of each other, not for Washington to steal from those in the country and give to others in the country." In response to a Democrat who invoked the Bible during the food stamp debate in Congress, Fincher cited his own biblical phrase: "The one who is unwilling to work shall not eat" (Stolberg 2013).[1] Fincher's remarks capture a presumed general truth that many accept, especially if there is no countervailing reason to believe otherwise. The presumed truth is that the recipients of assistance owe their food insecurity to individual choices, in particular, the choice not to work. The implicit assumption of Representative Fincher's remark is that federal assistance in the form of SNAP benefits rewards those who do not deserve this assistance. Those people who might qualify are either scamming the system by not looking for work, or they are lazy and unmotivated to find jobs. On either interpretation the remark is designed to impugn the moral character of those who need food assistance.[2] Perhaps it is clear enough that this kind of master narrative about *who is hungry and why* is damaging by virtue of morally denigrating a population of people. But there are other stories about food insecurity that do ethical damage but less obviously so.

Real stories of hunger

The stories I profile in this chapter are about women, in particular, because women are caretakers. Women assume a primary role in raising their grandchildren. They shoulder the responsibility for taking care of spouses who may suffer from chronic illness or disability, and they nurse an aging generation of parents and in-laws. This cultural role makes women most vulnerable to food insecurity since the expectation is that they will assume a disproportionate role in responding to the contingencies of living—accident, misfortune, illness, and death. Ironically, it seems as if we should celebrate the necessary role that some women undertake as caregivers. But stories about hungry women, in particular, also perpetuate the myth that hunger and food insecurity is produced by individual behavior, rather than by structural conditions, public policies, and political ideology.

Let me introduce you to some women who are food-insecure. They tell their own stories on the website, *Feeding America* ("Hunger in Your Community: Real Stories," n.d.). Amy is a divorced, single mom from Fresno, California. She was receiving food stamps to supplement her income but then she was injured at work and had to quit. Even though Amy qualified for SNAP benefits, the amount she received did not extend the whole month. So she found her way to the local food bank where she was able to supplement her benefits. There she met people she liked, and began to volunteer to help others in her community.

Mercedes, from Louisiana, recalled the day that tragedy struck her life; her daughter was killed. Now Mercedes is raising her grandchildren who range from two to fourteen years, including five-year-old twins. She says proudly that she "didn't ask for a dime" when she was working as a full-time caregiver. When she lost her job she hesitated to use the Second Harvest Food Bank because she felt ashamed. But then she realized that shame was not going to feed those six kids.

Roberta is from Mississippi where she worked for the state for thirty-one years, raised two children, and was looking forward to the "Golden Years" of retirement and leisure that she and her husband had planned. Instead they are now taking care of their three granddaughters, aged two, six, and eight. Roberta discovered that pensions and retirement income did not cover food and bills for her extended family. The local food pantry helps to make ends meet.

These stories are representative of a class of narratives about food insecurity. They have the following features in common: They are all told by the women themselves who are food-insecure, they illustrate how accidental misfortune (disability, illness, or death) contributes to the plight of food insecurity, and they reveal a lack of control over the causal conditions that create food insecurity.[3] Nonetheless, the stories suggest a solution. For the women who are hungry it is a local food shelf or food bank that solves their problems, at least temporarily. And for us, the consumers of these stories, what we can do is to donate our dollars or our time to charitable organizations that distribute free food. Of course, the use of "real stories" about hunger on the *Feeding America* website is calculated to produce a sympathetic response. We are more likely to donate if we know something particular about who is hungry and why. However, there is a high cost to using these kinds of stories to understand the problem of food insecurity. In the following section I make two criticisms of these stories—one about the characterization of food insecurity as accidental misfortune, and a second criticism that involves how the women narrators themselves are depicted. Their *ideal* agency, I argue, sets an unrealistically high standard for moral deservingness.

To begin it is significant that Amy, Mercedes, and Roberta explain their plight by alluding to contingencies or accidental misfortune. Amy refers to an injury that prevents her from working and Mercedes identifies the "tragic" death of her daughter, leaving Mercedes in charge of raising her grandchildren. Events like illness and death are sudden and incapacitating in their effects on ordinary ways of living. None of the hungry women profiled here can control these events. Nor is there is any evidence to suggest that their food insecurity is chronic or long lasting. In most cases their need to use the food pantry is only a temporary lapse in their efforts to work and provide for their families. Roberta, for example, is now back in school to get a degree to prepare for a new career that will allow her to support her three granddaughters (despite having already retired from a previous job). Because their cited reasons for being food-insecure are accidental, personal and idiosyncratic, readers shape their understanding of what counts as a solution to their respective plight(s) by reference to these articulated conditions. Temporarily making use of food banks and food pantries, for example, seems completely adequate to allow these hungry women to "get back on their feet." So what donors can and should be encouraged to do is to contribute more food or more money or more time to supporting food charity organizations that help women like Amy, Mercedes, and Roberta. In fact, this is a reasonable response since accidental misfortune is not something we should expect to protect against by changing laws, policies, or institutional arrangements. I will have more to say in Chapter 4 about what crucial background conditions are left out of these "real stories" about hunger.

There is an equally serious flaw in the kinds of stories I profile here, and that is the way they contribute to an unreasonably high standard of moral innocence. To see this notice first that the representative narratives from "Real Stories about Hunger" portray morally ideal women. These are women who step up to take care of extended family in an emergency when tragedy or misfortune strike. These women are strongly committed to improving their plight(s) by hard work or by increasing their earning potential. Amy, Mercedes, and Roberta all express their desire and willingness to work and their reluctance to depend on charitable food donations. Recall also that Mercedes declared that she was "ashamed" to receive donations of food. These virtuous character traits illustrate a strong work ethic and individualism about providing for one's own family. In particular, these stories about hungry women that profile accidental bad luck and misfortune suggest a kind of agency that is only temporarily curtailed. "I had no control over [my illness, losing my job, the death of my daughter]." "This event happened to me [like a natural disaster]." "I could not do otherwise [than to use the food bank]." "But still, my food insecurity is for the short term. I am now [working, working harder, getting a new degree and career]." "I am in charge of my life."

Here the standard of moral innocence (or virtue), and the temporary lack of control of women who tell their stories about hunger, sets an impossibly high standard for who deserves food charity. Not all cases of food insecurity can be forced into this paradigm of need. To see that this is so, consider those who are food-insecure and fail to meet the ideal standard implied by "Real Stories." Suppose we knew about any one of these hungry women that she was addicted to drugs or alcohol, was not willing to work menial jobs for less than minimum wage, was not trying very hard (or at all) to find work, attempted to buy nonfood items with her SNAP benefits, or was not being frugal in meal planning, purchasing, or the preparation of food. Worse, suppose she attempted to receive social services for more than she was qualified to receive, or that she was found guilty of a crime and convicted, or that she practiced prostitution, or that she was a member of a gang. Moral innocence can erode when we build certain kinds of background circumstances into a story about food insecurity. These circumstances can potentially challenge our conception about who morally deserves (or has the right) to access food. To put it another way, the *wrong* story about hungry women may effectively trump or interfere with our ideas about who has a fundamental right to be food secure. In this sense food justice is a fragile thing, depending as it does on the stories we tell about who is hungry and why.

The main cautionary point about the ideal women portrayed in *Real Stories* is that by only profiling these virtuous hungry women we risk contributing to the ideology of blaming the poor. We may come to believe that women like Amy, Mercedes, and Roberta do deserve food because they exhibit a sufficient degree of personal responsibility for their lives. Others may be classified as engaging in "deviant" behavior by making poor life choices (choosing not to work), engaging in wrongdoing, exhibiting moral vices, and so on. The ideology of blaming the poor for failures of personal responsibility is, in fact, reinforced when those who are food-insecure are depicted as morally pure. One way of responding to this problem is by challenging the standard of innocence itself. This is very much like the approach Meyers (2016) takes in her critical scrutiny of how victim paradigms shape the interpretation of victims' stories about human rights abuses.

Moral innocence and the "impure" victim

The concept of a victim of human rights abuse has its origins in the Geneva Conventions definition of refugees. From this Diana Tietjens Meyers (2016) distinguishes two victim paradigms: the "pathetic" victim and the "heroic" victim. The pathetic victim is characterized as someone who is innocent of wrongdoing relevant to their treatment, utterly helpless to resist this treatment, and someone who is subjected to "unspeakable suffering" (p. 32). Meyers notes that passivity and lack of agency have come to represent innocence, non-complicity, or blamelessness, all of which are important attributes of the victim necessary for justifying our compassion and ensuring that we see her as a victim of human rights abuse. This testimony at the Tribunal for the Former Yugoslavia captures the sense of the pathetic victim, in this case Bosnian women who endured trauma while present at the massacre of boys and men by Serb forces in Srebrenica in 1995: "This all took place in an atmosphere which was beyond their control; there was nothing they could have done. They were completely helpless" (p. 34).

The contrasting victim paradigm Meyers identifies is the "heroic victim" who is admired for her activism and strength of character, while at the same time the innocence of her agency is preserved. However, I am most interested in the more controversial concept of victimhood that Meyers refers to as "impure" victims. This way of classifying victims of human rights abuses characterizes them as courageous and not passive agents. But their choices and actions challenge the concept of innocence that operates in standard victim paradigms. Meyers uses the example of "smuggled" and trafficked sex workers who do not necessarily describe themselves as victims but rather as migrants who may have been deceived or coerced into accepting what they believed to be legal jobs abroad (Meyers 2016, 40). Anti-trafficking laws are ideally designed to protect sex workers who have been abused and exploited, bought and sold. But not all of these women easily satisfy the test of "innocence" since in some cases they have knowingly entered into jobs that have been promised to them, even though the conditions of employment have been falsely described and misrepresented. This leads Meyers to recommend a revision to the concept of agency that captures a less stringent criterion of innocence in victim paradigms. She calls this "burdened agency" in order to include the conditions of force, fraud, and coercion that constrain the choices and actions of trafficked sex workers (and others) (p. 62). For example, the most obvious way of understanding how *force* operates in the case of trafficked sex workers is to see that these women's choices are made in conditions of extreme poverty that create only a few desperate options.

> The stories that "smuggled" women tell feature alcoholic or absent husbands, children to support, jobs lost, deep debt, and rent payments in arrears (Waugh 2007; Pheterson 1989). What they aim to accomplish in handing themselves over to known thugs is to save themselves, their children, and sometimes their extended families from homelessness, chronic hunger, and other privations. (Meyers 2016, 43)

Meyers argues that the criterion of "innocence-as-passivity" is not consistent with "normal impurity of motivation" and the variety of strengths and weakness that allow individuals to negotiate the complexities of difficult lives. In other words, a person can still be a victim of human rights abuse even though she fails to meet the stringent standard of innocence assumed in the pathetic victim paradigm. As Meyers explains, the conditions of force, fraud, and coercion are norms that reasonable people will take into account that will not thereby disqualify sex workers as genuine victims of human rights abuse.

Meyers's criticism of the "innocence-as-passivity" standard in victim paradigms is enormously helpful for understanding narratives about food insecurity. In a similar way, the purported right to food may be trumped by challenges to the [moral] innocence of those who are hungry, as strange as this may seem given how fundamental food is to sustain all human lives. In order to correct this ideal standard of deservingness on display in "Real Stories about Hunger," we need a different kind of story about who is hungry and why. This is the main topic of Chapter 4. For now I can suggest in a qualified way what kinds of details should be included in such a story.

One feature of Meyers's criticism about the "innocence as passivity" standard is relatively undeveloped. When we make the judgment that conditions of force, fraud, or coercion apply in a particular case, we not only are mitigating blame for the victim. We are also identifying other background circumstances for moral review. For example, in the above descriptions of smuggled women who "voluntarily" enter into sex work, there are some agents who are doing the buying and selling, exploiting and oppressing, taking advantage of women by deceiving them and misrepresenting the conditions of work, or some husbands who are alcoholic and abusive, or some landlords who force women and their families into the streets. These circumstances are not morally neutral. They are conditions that on closer examination implicate individuals, institutions, governments, and so on, even as the contexts and targets of moral blame vary. The norms of force, fraud, and coercion function more widely than Meyers suggests since they not only operate to challenge the innocence standard of the pathetic victim paradigm. These norms direct our attention to the background conditions that explain the complexities of individual difficult lives, thereby enabling us to point to a proper target for moral wrongdoing (other than the victim of human rights abuse). We then can align this judgment about wrongdoing with our moral indignation about the constrained choices some women are forced to make (Ingram 2014). Likewise for those who may be classified as "impure victims" of food insecurity. Before we undertake the rewriting of hunger narratives in the next chapter it is instructive to look at one more context where storytelling is used to identify the needs of individuals and communities.

GlobalGiving

Please tell a story about a time when a person or organization tried to help someone or change something in your community.

One narrator from Kakemega, Kenya, responds by telling the following story titled "Assistance from the Red Cross":

> It was such miserable thing that happened to the community I stay with. There was hunger and many people died. Those who had animals had to sell them before hunger killed them. There was many people dying daily. Many people had to walk for long distances looking for water and food. Learning was interrupted due to severe famine and drought. An organization known as Red Cross came to help the victims. It was such a sigh relief when food was brought. The organization also drilled bore holes of which it has changed the economy in the country. Many people are now farmers which has boosted the economy. ("Storytelling Project—Turning Anecdotes into Useful Data," n.d. *GobalGiving*)

Another narrator from Kajiado, northeastern Kenya, tells a similar story titled "Famine":

> The rains have failed in all arid and semi-arid areas, the children drop out of school because of hunger. Other go hungry while other go work for other and

> get small which can take them only once meal in a day and night they go hungry. Livestock also die because they lack water and die green pastures. Wells, rivers, dams have run dried. Thanks to Red Cross for helping the people with donated food but still this food is not enough. ("Storytelling Project")

These and many other stories told in response to the open-ended question prompt above are part of the "storytelling project" undertaken by the nonprofit organization GlobalGiving. GlobalGiving matches donors with international development projects, partnering with many small grass roots organizations that seek to improve the quality of life for those who live in poverty, lack sufficient food or clean water, or face obstacles to education and employment ("About Us," n.d. *GlobalGiving*). According to their website, the storytelling project is a way that nonprofit organizations can effectively monitor and evaluate successes and failures of projects designed to help communities in need. Telling stories invites the beneficiaries themselves to articulate their needs and what is working (or not) in their communities. This allows GlobalGiving and their agency partners to fund projects initiated by members within the target community rather than from outside of it. Since 2010 the storytelling pilot program has collected over 10,000 stories about more than 250 different organizations working in Kenya ("Storytelling Project").

The analysis of these stories is crucial if they are to be effective in guiding development projects. To this end GlobalGiving has used the expertise of David Snowdon, the founder of the UK firm, Cognitive Edge. Snowdon utilizes software called "SenseMaker" to analyze large volumes of data that represent patterns of information produced by stories that cluster around features of meaning. To produce this kind of data, each storyteller locates a dot in a triangle that helps to contextualize what the story means. This is done by locating the dot closer to one point of the triangle identified as a "need," "solution," or as a "problem" (Boss 2011).

According to Snowdon, there are two features of this methodology that are important for its users. First is the idea that the storyteller is best qualified to interpret the meaning of the story. Second, the location of the dots on the triangular figure codifies nuances or shadings of contextual meaning from the narrator's point of view. When a large number of stories and their meanings are analyzed, the cluster of dots will reveal common elements that can helpfully guide development organizations to more directly and accurately target what a community needs (Boss 2011).

I will not try to assess how successful the storytelling project is for the nonprofit organizations that utilize this methodology. Rather, I want to draw attention to the way in which these kinds of stories contribute to our understanding about what counts as an appropriate solution to hunger and food insecurity. As before let's distinguish between charity and food justice, where the latter kind of solution seeks to change more fundamental structural conditions that disproportionately affect populations and subgroups. Does the storytelling project disclose what systemic unjust conditions need to change in order to address food insecurity? Not necessarily. On the one hand, the project makes it possible to hear authentic "voices" who contribute to an understanding of how things are from within local communities. But relying on the narrator's own understanding of local circumstances does not guarantee that these stories accurately identify causal and explanatory conditions that create problems of food insecurity in the first place. In other words, storytellers may misidentify or incorrectly describe *why* members of their communities experience famine and hunger. Perhaps it is explained by drought, as one of our narrators suggests. But perhaps also there are more systemic failures by governments, institutions, or policies that contribute to worsening quality of life and increased hunger and poverty in particular communities. Of course, we cannot expect that those participants who respond to the general question prompt are privy to this macro-perspective that includes more general causal and structural conditions. This is not the fault of the storyteller herself. Narrators may well misrepresent what kinds of solutions to hunger are appropriate because the relevant background conditions are, to a large extent, opaque to them from their own perspective. Call this the "epistemic obstacle" in the storytelling project.

We can get a sense of the epistemic obstacle at work by looking more closely at the two representative stories included here. Both storytellers write about hunger in their respective communities in Kenya. And both stories are about the charitable food donations by the organization, Red Cross of Kenya. But how these charitable donations are depicted is different when the contextual meanings are included. The author of "Assistance" identifies these donations as a "solution" to hunger while the author of "Famine" identifies the Red Cross donations as somewhere between a "need" and a "problem." But which is it? It is not as though one storyteller's interpretation is right and the other is wrong and needs to be corrected. But according to GlobalGiving, the stories purportedly help nonprofit organizations identify the accurate conditions of need in local communities:

> Social challenges are complex. Intertwined root causes affect infant mortality, unemployment, malnutrition, etc. How can organizations pinpoint and provide solutions to communities' most pressing needs? ("Storytelling Project")

Because social challenges—as well as identifying the root causes of food insecurity—*are* complex, it should not be expected that individual storytellers could overcome the epistemic obstacle in order to identify and recommend systemic and structural changes as more permanent and sustainable solutions to hunger. Here it seems clear that food justice should not depend merely on the point of view of the recipients of charity and the stories they tell.[4]

Feeding the nonprofits

It might be argued that I expect too much of the stories I criticize above. After all, these stories are the public faces of charities and nonprofit development organizations that seek donations and funding to continue their missions to help those in need. So, of course, they champion the kind of story that ensures the outcome they desire—more donations. And if a particular kind of story does successfully inspire some of us to donate time or money to charitable organizations that feed the hungry, then this not cause for complaint (or so the objection might go).

In reply I want to first situate the use of stories within a larger framework to give the reader a sense of the wide variety of ways in which organizations use storytelling to advance their respective interests and causes. In "Digital Storytelling for Social Impact," Jay Geneske (n.d.) describes the practice of storytelling as a "means to improve the well-being of the poor and vulnerable around the world." Philanthropic organizations, businesses, and nonprofits can all benefit from the storytelling culture. And, in fact, the Rockefeller Foundation has funded a number of organizations (including GlobalGiving) to undertake initiatives that utilize best practices of storytelling. These tips, guidelines, and case studies about storytelling can be found on the website titled *Hatch for Good* ("Tell Stories with Purpose," n.d.). Here we find a classification of the kinds of stories nonprofits should be telling: values and ethics stories, social proof stories, founder stories, continuous improvement stories, and impact stories. In addition, recommendations about content suggest profiling the organization's cause, the problems targeted by the organization, and the solutions that give hope and include a call to action. One tip advises, "Begin each story with a message or image about the people affected by your work that encourages the audience to like and respect them. Ideally, the audience should see themselves—or people they aspire to be—in the story." The website also includes links to case studies, for example, organizations such as UNICEF, The Gates Foundation, and Greenpeace, which have used storytelling to good effect to advance their respective causes and to broadcast their stories to a wide audience using social media like Twitter, Facebook, and Instagram ("Tell Stories with Purpose").

This widespread interest in the practice of storytelling suggests that narratives may function rather successfully to advance and sustain the respective causes of development organizations to advertise their work. In this respect the story may align with food justice outcomes or not, depending on the goals and mission of the organization that articulates the story. In other words, when narratives function in the way that is recommended by Hatch for Good, the narrative is *at the service* of the organization. So if the goal of a particular nonprofit is charitable giving, then in all probability the story written by that organization will profile charity as a solution to food insecurity. But this is not the only way to use stories. Since one of the explicitly stated objectives for telling a good story is to describe the problems of communities in need, there is surely the potential to improve a story in such a way that it discloses more fundamental structural conditions that contribute to explaining why a population is food-insecure, as well as to propose sustainable solutions beyond charitable giving. In other words, the right [food justice] story can and should have conceptual priority over the mission of any particular nonprofit organization. The story is not *at the service* of development organizations, it is the other way around. Sustainable solutions to hunger are responsive to accurate descriptions about the structural conditions that cause food insecurity in the first place. So these background conditions need to be on display in the narrative itself.

By promoting digital storytelling for social impact we risk too narrowly defining the function of storytelling as *merely* a method to inspire donations and promote an organization's mission. In fact, stories that profile the needs of individuals and communities are consumed by a large audience who shape their ideas about how best to solve food insecurity and global poverty. So there is the potential for misrepresenting the proximate causes and explanatory conditions of food insecurity to the general public, and not merely to targeted potential donors. And when we do so misrepresent why a population is food-insecure, there is a greater risk of getting the solution wrong as well.

One further impediment to telling a more accurate story about why a population is food-insecure is that the political ideology of some nonprofit organizations may be resistant to the articulation of structural conditions as causes of poverty and inequality. As we have seen, one pernicious belief about those who live in poverty is that the poor alone are personally responsible for their plight, as well as personally responsible for overcoming their predicament by changing presumed dysfunctional behavior, working harder, or becoming more self-reliant. According to Erica Kohl-Arenas (2015) this "self-help myth" is currently alive and well, shaping the way in which philanthropic organizations manage their dollars, and defining the way in which community organizations identify their needs as well as the kinds of grass roots initiatives that are possible to fund. We learn exactly how this happens by Kohl-Arenas's analysis of philanthropic organizations that are seemingly devoted to improving the quality of life for farmworkers and immigrants who work in industrial agricultural in California's Central Valley. Here farmworkers still face "enduring poverty" from low-paying jobs, and struggle to overcome overt discrimination, food insecurity, poor health, substandard housing (no heat or clean running water), and dangerous working conditions such as exposure to heavy pesticide use. Yet private philanthropic foundations perpetuate systems of inequality that create and sustain poverty for these populations of workers by endorsing some variation of the self-help myth, and by ignoring the "root causes" of poverty; those attributable to structural inequalities created by industrial agriculture such as, "an agricultural system that relies on continuing waves of seasonal low-wage migrant labor; stalled immigration reform; and the historically racist power structure in the region" (Kohl-Arenas 2016, 77).

One crucial insight that emerges from Kohl-Arenas's analysis is that grass roots organizers and nonprofit organizational staff are sometimes forced to negotiate, interpret, defy, or subvert the conservative agendas of funding organizations in order to advance activist initiatives that challenge dominant power structures. As we learn also, a central dilemma or "contradiction" of self-help philanthropy is that activism on behalf of farmworkers and immigrant labor actually threatens the social and economic infrastructures of foundation organizations that fund such nonprofits. Since nonprofit funding organizations are often supported by surplus capital that is the result of wealth acquired at the expense of low-wage workers, one might wonder whether or not this contradiction is a permanent and intractable problem about nonprofit funding organizations. As one program officer who was interviewed by Kohl-Arenas says, "I would never attempt to bring a grant proposal to my board that speaks of challenging economic inequity through direct action organizing, labor or welfare rights, or holding businesses or major industries such as agriculture accountable. Such proposals have been known to cost many a program officer their jobs" (p. 91). This kind of remark testifies to how unrealistic it may be to expect nonprofit organizations to tell a certain kind of story about hunger and poverty—one that discloses and implicates power structures that produce food insecurity by contributing to the oppression, marginalization, and economic exploitation of those who labor to produce our food (Dixon 2016).

Conclusion

Where are we so far? I have tried to identify the high cost of using master narratives about food insecurity to shape more sustainable justice solutions to hunger. In one kind of case the implication is that anyone who needs food assistance is morally flawed. Here the pernicious assumption is that food insecurity is produced by choices to "get something for nothing," or by choosing not to work from laziness. Alternatively, the website Feeding America profiles individuals who suffer from temporary and accidental misfortune who are forced to rely on local food shelves. I have argued that this kind of story misrepresents the root causes of poverty and hunger by emphasizing the contingencies of living that cannot be controlled, predicted, or protected against. The only reasonable solution to hungry women described in this way is to offer charity in temporary doses. As well, these representative *real stories* set an impossibly high standard of moral innocence and deservingness that cannot be met by the larger population of those who are food-insecure. One way of correcting for these problems is to include a deeper contextual analysis of those circumstances that create deprivation of opportunity for individuals and populations. Then we are better positioned to evaluate the presence of mitigating factors that constrain choices for a larger class of those who are food-insecure, as well as to recommend what more systemic conditions need to change as a matter of justice.

A similar problem emerges from the storytelling project used by the development organization, GlobalGiving. This narrative methodology also relies on those who are poor and hungry to articulate their condition(s) of need. While this kind of story ensures that individuals can give voice to their concerns, it does not guarantee that these narrators will accurately identify and describe systemic injustices that create or entrench poverty and food insecurity in the first place. In fact, as we saw in the two sample stories above, some storytellers might be well satisfied with charitable donations as a solution that meets their immediate needs, as opposed to more sustainable justice solutions to food insecurity.

Now that we have identified some particular problems created by damaging master narratives about who is hungry and why, it is time to consider exactly how a food justice narrative resists the ethical damage created by these master narratives. In the next chapter I argue that we can effectively do so by *rewriting* the call to charity.

Mother Hubbard's Cupboard: Food Bank

I stood outside the entry to the main Food Bank distribution center in Bloomington. I was waiting for our crew from Mother Hubbard, and the truck used to transport food from this main site to our own food pantry downtown. Our job as "shoppers" is to find what is on offer for that day, load it up on carts, line it up to be weighed or checked off by the directors of the Food Bank, load it onto our truck, and then unload it at the food pantry. We were not the only organization poking around looking for food. Other groups arrived at the same time with vans or small trucks. Some of these were church groups or charitable organizations, but in a way we were all competing with one another for the "good stuff."

"The good stuff does not include cookies, pop tarts, or sugary cereals," Erin told me as she was guiding me around pointing to bins, boxes, and crates. In the dry food section there were huge crates of canned goods. One of my jobs was to paw through these to find something that counted as protein or that was not loaded with salt. "Look for something exceptional," Erin said over her shoulder as she left me to load about 133 pounds of canned goods into five plastic crates. These instructions invited some interpretation on my part. I decided that canned green beans and corn did not qualify as exceptional. Why were there so many of these kinds of vegetables? But I did snag chickpeas, black beans, tuna, a large container of chicken meat, and artichoke hearts, as well as tomatoes and chili. I scored a major find in a box of dry goods that contained about twenty large packages of whole almonds.

The dry section of the food bank is only one part of our load today. Patrick was busy in the cooler locating yogurt, milk, juices, and tofu products. These were carefully selected by dates and loaded on separate carts. If the due date has passed, then the MHC is not charged for these products. But, of course, if the date is too far-gone then the product is no good to us or to anyone. A flat of milk we looked at shopping on October 15 was stamped, "Do not sell after September 25th." We left it in the cooler. Then there is the frozen food cooler. Today we snatched up a whole cart (sixteen boxes) of "food share" products. These are dinner type foods, some cooked, like lasagna, pizzas, or burritos that local restaurants have donated. The food is repackaged in plastic by the Food Bank, labeled, and boxed for organizations like ours. These are very popular I was told. And, looking at the offerings I could see why—gourmet food, ready to eat.

My first day shopping at the Food Bank was disorienting. Luckily, I had Patrick to guide me around. Patrick is efficient, knowledgeable, and completely fun; a free spirit let loose among donated food. He did ask my advice on the various credentials of yogurt brands since, he confessed, does not eat it himself. But this is a person who knows his way around a food bank. First stop. Grab a cart. Today we needed four or five of these to load our goods and move them to the truck. Patrick knew we would be stuck waiting for everyone else to finish if we did not do this one simple thing first. He is not all business though. There is always something to make Patrick laugh. Between loading the carts he shoots baskets into the hoop set up above the door to the cooler. When the food is all loaded, high fives all around. "Yes! Look at this truck! What a beautiful job you did loading this truck," Patrick tells me slapping me on the back. "Great job!" When we meet at MHC's food pantry where the food is actually distributed to customers five days a week, we reverse the process and lug boxes, crates, and flats into the building, and snug them into cold and dry storage areas. Volunteers coming later today will organize all the new products, making sure the older stuff gets on the shelves first. But for now we are finished. Other food will be delivered right to the pantry three more times this week in addition to another scheduled shopping trip to the Food Bank. Wow. A lot of food coming in and going out.

I still want to know more about the people I am working with. But I am also concentrating on being a good worker so maybe those conversations will have to come later.

4

Rewriting the Call to Charity

The sign above the entrance to the Interfaith Food Shelf reads, "I was hungry and you gave me food." There is no doubt that this religious evocation is inspirational for most of the volunteers who help distribute emergency food to members of our local community. But this simple call to charity also blinds us to certain facts about food justice. First, it leaves out why these individuals who visit the food shelf are hungry. Second, it suggests that the generous volunteers who staff the food shelf (and others) have met their political responsibilities by engaging in charity work. But as Young (2011, 73) argues, the issue of our respective responsibility for justice is more complicated:

> We should also ask whether and how we contribute by our actions to structural processes that produce vulnerabilities to deprivation and domination for some people who find themselves in certain positions with limited options compared to others.

If Young's argument that individual citizens have a responsibility to alleviate social and political injustice is plausible, then we should ask how best to position the volunteer epistemically. One obstacle that interferes with transforming ordinary citizens into policy advocates is lack of knowledge about systemic injustices that unequally oppress and constrain the choices of individuals who are attempting to live well. In this chapter I argue that what we need is a new practical strategy for revealing the structural conditions that more fundamentally explain the causes of poverty and hunger. This strategy involves using *food justice narratives* that profile those who are food-insecure and include descriptions of social, political, and economic background conditions of more than one person. To this end I borrow the concept of a counterstory (Nelson 2001). By reading, watching, or even writing a counterstory, the volunteer or ordinary citizen becomes alert to a way of seeing structural inequalities that locate some groups of people to unfair disadvantage. Acquiring this point of view is necessary for undertaking our collective responsibilities for achieving food justice because it positions us to see what structural conditions must change.

The food justice lens

The tensions existing between food justice advocates and hunger relief advocates are well documented in much of the literature about alternative food movements. For example, Gottlieb and Joshi (2010) identify the need to describe hunger as an issue about economic justice in such a way as to transform earnest and motivated food shelf volunteers into policy advocates. Winne (2008) and Holt Giménez (2011b) both urge an alliance between the charity worker and the food justice advocate. In particular, Winne laments that even though food banks and charity work attract the attention of many influential people, rarely do those people participate in public policy discourse about poverty and hunger. Holt-Giménez (2011b, 319) remarks that, "Where one stands on hunger depends on where one sits." He recommends a "radical" approach to food justice issues that targets structural changes in the food system, creating opportunities for increased equity in land ownership and working towards a redistribution of wealth. But as Holt-Giménez reminds us, what we also need in order to advance such large-scale systematic policy changes are coalitions between those who are working for underserved populations, and those who are directly involved with the structural transformation of our food system. Allen (2010) suggests that local food movements can aspire to food justice goals by (a) increasing understanding of structural conditions, (b) analyzing local food priorities and activities, and (c) evaluating criteria for social justice. She also emphasizes the need for structural change in the form of public policy, urging the importance of changing beliefs and attitudes to work towards social change by developing a sense of "critical consciousness." Allen and Guthman (2006) claim that the priority of alternative food movements must involve changing policies and economic patterns rather than merely making better personal choices. Guthman (2008) urges more structural activism about inequity. What will facilitate this shift in focus in the direction of social and political change? Guthman recommends that we move toward a politics of "listening, watching, and not always helping" (p. 443). Sbicca's (2012) case study of People's Grocery examines how this food justice organization addresses food justice goals in order to mobilize volunteers to target the structural causes of hunger and poverty. Sbicca's research reveals that one problem facing People's Grocery, in particular, is finding an ideological underpinning to support the mobilization of these activists' efforts. Hassanein (2003) argues persuasively that to achieve even incremental change in the food system requires the method of food democracy, which depends on an informed citizenry and a deeper engagement by ordinary citizens. Gilson (2014) argues that the citizen-consumer has political responsibilities for food justice beyond merely "voting with her fork." These responsibilities extend to "interrogating the political-economic structures that are part of the normal conditions of the industrial, global food system." But in order to envision what ought to be done, ordinary citizens need also to reevaluate assumptions about personal responsibility.

The need for political and structural change to address food insecurity is clearly identified by all of these writers. But we might still want to know *how* to implement these suggestions practically in order to increase understanding of structural conditions, or *how best* ordinary citizens should become informed, or *how* they will develop a critical consciousness. One overlooked aspect of the food justice lens is determining what ordinary citizens should know in order to develop tactics and strategies for bringing about food justice. This is an epistemic obstacle that must be overcome before we can expect that volunteers at the food pantry, for example, can transform into policy advocates. This is especially problematic for those who do charity work on behalf of the hungry since they must be able to see beyond the culturally entrenched idea that charity is the solution to hunger. Poppendieck (1998) describes the "moral safety valve" function of charitable organizations that feed the hungry, which is the idea that by donating time, food, or money to various kinds of emergency food programs, we relieve ourselves of the need to work on changing the more fundamental causes of poverty.[1]

If we explain food insecurity by reference to the failure of individual responsibility, then we are more likely to ignore the background conditions that contextualize circumstances that constrain individual choice and action. And if these background conditions are obscured then it is much more difficult to identify what needs to be done in order to correct these systemic injustices. In other words, it is unlikely that we will seek to change systemic and structural conditions of poverty and hunger if we cannot see or identify these structural causes in the first place, as well as how these causes unjustly operate to disadvantage certain populations.

But what conditions are structural? And what counts as structural injustice? According to Young (2011), structural injustice differs from two other types of injury. A person may be wronged by actions perpetrated by other individuals, as when a person's integrity or self-esteem is harmed by a racist comment or a woman is denied employment because of sexist attitudes by someone in a position of authority. Alternatively, a person may be harmed by a specific action or policy implemented by states or institutions. For example, if that person is denied employment because of her age and there is a corporate policy that institutionalizes age discrimination, then she is wronged by an unjust corporate policy. But Young insists that structural injustices do not reduce to either of these kinds of wrongs. Structural injustices create conditions of vulnerability for individuals by virtue of the social structural position these individuals occupy. To understand structural injustice requires us to take a "macro" view of society where we attempt to bring into focus some general conditions that operate on individuals with diverse life histories, attributes, and goals (p. 56). These complex conditions are attributable to many individuals as well as to public and private institutional policies. The salient feature of these sets of social circumstances is that they operate according to "normal rules and accepted practices" to create vulnerabilities and disadvantages for subgroups (p. 52). The practical problem I address in the next section is how to convey these kinds of structural background conditions about poverty and hunger to ordinary citizens, including the charity worker. The vehicle for doing so is a food justice narrative that profiles those structural conditions which create food insecurity.

Case study: *A Place at the Table*

From this perspective let us return to the stories we tell about individual people who are vulnerable specifically to food insecurity. What is it about these stories that will enable us to see how structural injustices operate? One example is the popular documentary film, *A Place at the Table* (Jacobson and Silverbush 2013), which includes several stories of people who experience some degree of food insecurity. One story introduces Barbie, a single mother of two young children in Philadelphia who actively searches for work after losing her job. She aspires to attend college for training and to increase her earning potential, but realizes how impossible this goal is for her now. Her immediate urgent problem is to feed herself and her children. She relies on public assistance to do so, including food stamps, food pantries, and free meal programs for her children. But even so she is barely making ends meet, even when she is eventually employed full-time at a job that pays US$ 9 per hour. It seems that being employed at this wage creates further obstacles. Barbie is now US$ 2 over the monthly income limit for food stamp eligibility, and her children no longer qualify for the free meal programs they received when she was not working at all.

Why does Barbie's story qualify as a food justice narrative? Telling Barbie's story in this particular way defies some assumptions about why she is food-insecure. Barbie wants to work and she eventually gets a full-time job. So she hardly fits Rep. Fincher's description of a person who is "unwilling to work." Moreover, Barbie's food insecurity is not due to bad luck, misfortune, or some idiosyncratic temporary lapse in her personal responsibility to support herself and her children. The background conditions that the filmmakers use to explain her food insecurity are systemic and structural. They include lack of accessible food or nearby fully stocked supermarkets, difficult and lengthy travel to find these cheaper food markets, low-wage pay scale, eligibility limits for receiving SNAP benefits, and qualifying income levels for children's free meal programs. What the audience of this film should notice is that these conditions operate collectively to disadvantage Barbie and others who occupy the same generalized position (single mothers, low-income families, etc.). But no one law or policy is actually designed to harm. In fact, social services are designed to help people like Barbie who are struggling. Even so, the obstacles that constrain Barbie's choices combine to disadvantage her, and these circumstances are beyond her individual ability to control.

Barbie's lack of agential control is not created by contingent circumstances of ill health or accident, unlike the stories about Amy, Mercedes, and Roberta in Chapter 3. Rather, it is owed to systemic conditions that she cannot change no matter how hard she tries. For example, the filmmakers direct our attention to other background conditions such as US Department of Agriculture (USDA) subsidies and lobbying. We learn, for example, that 84 percent of USDA subsidies have gone to mega-farms and agribusiness to support commodity crops such as corn, cotton, soy, wheat, and rice. Not coincidentally, in 2011 agribusiness spent US$ 124.7 million in special interest lobbying, outspent only by oil and gas corporations. As Congress has continued to support the large corporate food industry, it has also gradually decreased funding programs—including SNAP benefits, National School Lunch, housing subsidies, programs for seniors, and Aid to Families with Dependent Children (AFDC)—that support those living at the margins of society (Jacobson and Silverbush 2013).

Telling Barbie's story together with this explanatory context directs the viewer's attention to more systemic conditions that are complex, large-scale, and attributable to many individuals, institutions, and public policies. Despite the complexity of this macro view of food insecurity, at least the background conditions are sufficiently articulated so that we can inquire about their ethical justifiability. The deeper and fuller story of hunger revealed by this food justice narrative makes it possible to ask, "What social and political conditions should change?"

Blaming the poor

What is less clearly challenged in this example of a food justice narrative is the standard of moral innocence that typically characterizes who is hungry. In the same way that the *Feeding America* website depicts ideal food-insecure storytellers like Amy, Mercedes, and Roberta, Barbie and the other characters profiled in *A Place at the Table* are ideal in the sense that they are industrious and willing to work. That is, they each occupy socially acceptable professions: rancher, grill cook, schoolchild, and police officer. The filmmakers seem to have followed the "tip" for good storytelling proposed on the website Hatch for Good: "Begin each story with a message or image about the people affected by your work that encourages the audience to like and respect them. Ideally, the audience should see themselves—or people they aspire to be—in the story" ("Tell Stories with Purpose," n.d. *Hatch for Good*). The problem with invoking this ideal standard for who is hungry is that many other food-insecure individuals are "less than pure." Because they do not meet the test for moral innocence they may be thought undeserving of the right to food. This matters because the right to food is a fundamental right; it applies to all humans regardless of their circumstances. But when someone who is food-insecure is blamed for wrongdoing, this may contribute to impugning her moral character. In these cases our moral appraisal of the person may well interfere with recognizing her basic right to food.

To address this concern we might make use of Erin Kelly's (2013) account of blame to distinguish between judgments about wrongdoing, and judgments about unfair circumstances of living that constrain choices and opportunities to act. Kelly suggests that our blaming practices are a collection of "reactive attitudes" including resentment, indignation, and retributive behavior that are responses to a person's wrongdoing. These attitudes also signal moral criticism of the person who commits the wrong action. "Blame points to a person's moral unreliability and traces it to a standing aspect of his or her character, dispositions, or personhood" (p. 246). But Kelly's main argument is to deny that blame reduces to appraisals of wrongdoing. Rather, judgments about blame and wrongdoing sometimes "pull apart." In these kinds of cases we require different norms for judging that an individual has done something morally or legally wrong, as distinct from the practice of blaming this person. For example, even though killing one's spouse counts as a wrong action, we may vary our moral blame depending on the circumstances: killing him to get his money versus killing him to protect herself from further abuse and battering. In both cases we acknowledge wrongdoing, but we moderate the degree of moral blame we believe the agent deserves depending on the agent's reasons and motivations for killing the spouse.

The norm of blameworthiness Kelly recommends involves assessing "how reasonable it is to expect an agent to act morally in the face of obstacles" (2013, 256). In some cases we may judge that a moral agent faces contingencies of living that unfairly burden her and which create difficult circumstances that make the demands and expectations of morality unreasonably hard to meet. In these cases compassion is the appropriate response. What then counts as a moral excuse that mitigates blame? Background conditions that create significant obstacles to living include, for example, being forced into prostitution by poverty, or being unemployed because the company has laid off workers. According to Kelly, excuses that mitigate blame come in degrees, vary contextually, signal judgments of unfairness about the agent's circumstances, and are connected to compassion (p. 258). Compassion, in particular, is central to learning to see instances of injustice since stories that engage us emotionally can potentially educate our moral judgments. As Kelly remarks, even though we may judge that an individual has acted in a morally troubling way, the attitude of compassion "softens the connection between the agent and her wrongful act" (p. 261).[2]

What if obstacles to living rightly are created by an agent's own morally flawed behavior? Suppose a person is destitute because he gambled away his life savings, or suppose he is homeless (and hungry) because he has used all his money to buy drugs. If so, then these circumstances may fail to inspire our compassion, and we may resist seeing these contextual details as moral excuses for which the agent should not be blamed (Kelly 2013, 249). Kelly responds to this objection by maintaining that we can still scrutinize the deeper historical circumstances of living to ask whether or not the agent's actions were constrained, forced, or could have been avoided. The likely "forces" may be attributable to addiction or poverty, she adds.

One reason for invoking Kelly's account of blame is to challenge the ideal standard of hungry women that we see depicted in stories profiled by some hunger relief organizations. The norms for blameworthiness suggested by Kelly instruct us about how to mitigate blame for those who are "less pure" victims of food insecurity. But this is only a partial rationale. My main concern is more general since it points to the importance of including contextual details in stories about food justice. The kind of context that should be included in a food justice narrative includes background conditions that disadvantage populations of people, and not only individuals. These are structural conditions that qualify as oppressive, exploitative, or marginalizing. Here we will be looking for patterns or generalities that explain how the failure to nourish oneself is owed to limited choices and deprivation of opportunities. Without seeing these background circumstances in a story we may come to mistakenly believe that food insecurity is an individual failing—a failing of personal responsibility. And, most importantly, we may fail to see that a solution to hungry women requires structural and institutional change, and not merely charity, fortitude, and hard work.

Case study: The Hunger Project

In Chapter 3 I identified a difficulty with the storytelling project used by the organization GlobalGiving. I called this the "epistemic obstacle." In some cases a story about a community's need is articulated by individuals from within that community by responding to a general question prompt—*Please tell a story about a time when a person or organization tried to help someone or change something in your community*. But as I argued earlier there is no guarantee that the story that is told will identify and describe more fundamental structural conditions that contribute to why a community, state, or country is food-insecure. This is not the fault of the narrator, per se, because we cannot expect that individuals who reply to this question prompt can see or understand all of the relevant contextual details that matter to an accurate explanation of food insecurity in their own communities. The general problem here is not only the failure to include background context in the content of the narrative, but also how it is being used. When development organizations use narratives to identify problems and subsequent solutions to food insecurity, these narratives function at the service of the organization. So if the mission of a particular organization is charitable giving, then in all probability this organization will employ stories to encourage charity as a solution to food insecurity. I suggested in the previous chapter that development organizations should be at the service of a food justice narrative, and not the other way around. So what should we look for in a food justice narrative that is more correctly employed by nonprofit development organizations?

The success stories found on the website of the global organization, The Hunger Project, identify particular women who have benefitted from the skill training and resources of this nonprofit in 24,000 communities throughout Africa, South Asia and Latin America ("Stories of Success," n.d. *The Hunger Project*).[3] One woman profiled is Sankura Slamata who lives in Burkina Faso. She recently organized a market garden for women to grow vegetables during the dry season—cabbage, onions, sorrel, tomatoes, and okra. This was made possible by working alongside Boulkon Epicenter's credit community of the Hunger Project–Burkina Faso. This local community organization educates women in microcredit management, and trains them in activities that generate income. The market garden sells their produce to local markets and benefits these women who participate by contributing to their earnings and by making nutritional food more accessible.[4]

Rejeya Khatun is from Naopara, a village in the Meherpur district of Bangladesh. Rejeya is newly married but her husband was not employed, so the family struggled to eat. A friend advised her to get involved with a Hunger Project sponsored group called, Participatory Action Research. This group provided Rejeya with six months of skills training to learn how to sew and tailor. Now she takes orders for small jobs, works full time, and even participates in training other women to do similar work. This additional income provides Rejeya with many benefits. She is raising her daughter with adequate food, but also the family now has access to health care and is living in a good environment ("Stories of Success").

These success stories describe what particular women have done to improve their lives with the help of projects and initiatives funded by The Hunger Project. Because the stories do not rely on the individual narrator to articulate her need or the problems her community faces, the stories circumvent the epistemic obstacle. But from the stories we still understand something about what more basic resources are needed by the storyteller to improve her life. Sankura has increased access to nutritional food because she grows and sells from a community market garden. But we learn that this was made possible by a local system of microcredit loans that enabled her to organize the garden, invest in seeds or plants, train other women to participate, and sell the produce to members of the community. Rejeya began to work full time sewing and tailoring only because she participated in a skills program sponsored by The Hunger Project. So even though each woman profiled in these success stories manifests initiative and hard work, their success is not depicted as the result of merely taking personal responsibility for providing food for themselves and their families. Instead the stories point the reader to an understanding of more systemic conditions that must change in order to address "*sustainable* progress in overcoming hunger and poverty." These targeted issues identified by The Hunger Project include the following: empowering girls to have opportunities to be educated and healthy, addressing environmental problems, correcting gender discrimination that unequally impedes opportunities to work or to be educated, improving health (HIV/AIDS), increasing access to nutritional food, partnering with local political institutions, improving nutrition and access to clean water and better sanitation, and addressing poverty and food prices.[5] These are structural conditions that the organization profiles as central to creating sustainable solutions to global hunger.

Consider, specifically, how this nonprofit explains the need to address gender discrimination. The link directing the reader to this issue tells us that even though women make up 70 percent of agricultural labor, they still represent 60 percent of the world's hungry. Women face limitations on access to agricultural inputs, credit services and markets to sell products. They lack economic power and opportunities to education and access to basic healthcare. But when women do have the opportunity to generate and control an income, they invest in food, healthcare and education for themselves and their families. The particular Hunger Project programs that target gender discrimination include ways to empower women to be self-reliant and to assume leadership roles in their local communities as well as to participate in local, regional and national legislation. These programs include microfinance programs and skills training for women to start businesses, Strengthening Women's Leadership in Election Processes (SWEEP), Women Empowerment Program (WEP), empowering girl children in Bangladesh, HIV/AIDS educational workshops to halt the spread of disease, etc.

Remember Amy, Roberta, and Mercedes who tell their stories on the Feeding America website? They each characterize their dilemma of food insecurity as something they have no control over because it is due to contingencies of living that cannot be anticipated or changed. The solutions that are available to Amy, Roberta, and Mercedes require their own individual abilities and talents to overcome what is only a temporary condition. In contrast, The Hunger Project supplies the attentive reader with a more accurate depiction of what systemic conditions need to change as this is articulated by the goals and objectives of the organization itself. By identifying and describing what women need in order to improve their quality of life we gain a more complete picture of the problem of food insecurity. We also see what kinds of solutions are sustainable when these are reflected in the success stories of particular women.

A food justice narrative functions as a counterstory by satisfying two conditions. First, it should "resist" those damaging master narratives that distort or misrepresent who is hungry and why. Second, a food justice narrative should position ordinary citizens epistemically to identify structural injustices that contribute to food insecurity, especially those conditions of poverty and income inequality that disadvantage populations of people (women, single mothers, children, or working families). This positioning of the reader is achieved by rewriting the story about hunger in such a way that we can identify more sustainable justice solutions to food insecurity beyond the call to charity. So the *narrative act* (what is done with the story) is to reveal what is hidden by master narratives about hunger. In this way we position the reader or viewer to see those background conditions that create structural injustice in order to identify what must change to achieve food justice.

In order for a food justice narrative to contribute to the skill development of the ethical novice, it should satisfy three additional conditions: particularity, accuracy, and emotional engagement. Certainly the stories from the documentary film, *A Place at the Table* and The Hunger Project website are about particular people who suffer from food insecurity. This is what informs us about how real people suffer and struggle to nourish themselves. However, the narrators of the film, as well as the development organization, situate these particular lives in a larger social, political, and economic setting. This satisfies the accuracy condition. Barbie is not food-insecure because of poor choices or bad behavior. Rejeya is not struggling to feed her family because she does not want to work or because she is ill as a matter of bad luck. Each woman occupies a position that represents the plight of other single mothers, or mothers of families where there is no work available, or where there are no opportunities to gain skills or an education to improve the capacity to earn a livable wage. It is these background conditions that contribute to seeing how structural conditions unequally disadvantage these particular women and the social groups they represent. Barbie wants to go to college. But then she realizes that her children are hungry right now. How will she pay for this and support her children? This opportunity is closed to her but not for reasons attributable to an individual failure of agency, motivation, or responsibility. The film positions the viewer to construe this deprivation as a structural injustice, set against the background of political machinations that lead to decreased funding for AFDC, SNAP benefits, and the National School Lunch Program.

What about the capacity of the story to move us emotionally? Recall that to engage our emotions the story must depict individuals whose lives we care about. And, in order for the story to educate our emotions it should guide our feelings to see instances of injustice more perspicuously. I will return to Barbie as an example of how this condition is satisfied because she appears in several different settings displaying a range of emotions. When we first meet her Barbie is struggling but resigned to the task of trying to gather food for herself and her two children. Later when she does find permanent work there is a kind of joyfulness that buoys her along. And we, the viewers, also feel how great it is for her to finally have a job and a regular paycheck. Ultimately this disqualifies her from SNAP benefits and the free lunch program her children have been receiving. Until this moment Barbie has seemed resilient and strong. But then we see her tears and her vulnerability to the relentless predicament of affording food for herself and her children. Understanding why she is in this position is key. The tears are a display of hopelessness about conditions that she wants to desperately change but cannot. And the viewer feels the same despair. The new perspective achieved is what it means to be hungry in this unceasing way. This is not a temporary emotional crisis but a chronic despondency. Then, again, when we watch Barbie speaking about poverty and hunger to members of Congress she is proud, dignified, and impassioned. We also share this public moment with her and the emotions she is feeling. It is not merely that she appears to be like we are; it is that her emotions signal to us what it means to be vulnerable to a system that unequally disadvantages her and other single mothers. What we feel is moral indignation directed towards institutional failings and a lack of will on the part of government to create policies that meet the needs of ordinary women like Barbie. This is how our emotions are educated to see what is structurally unjust in this particular food justice narrative.

Conclusion

Today the editors of our local newspaper awarded a public "cheer" to the owner of a laundromat and car wash ("Cheers and Jeers," 2014). The owner was commended because he treated a homeless man with respect, "a gesture that other people may not have been able to muster." The owner also gave the homeless man a US$ 1 token for being a good customer. The editors concluded, "It was a small gesture but an important one, maintaining the dignity of the homeless man. Wouldn't it be wonderful if everyone treated less fortunate people with kindness and compassion instead of disdain?" (p. A5). Two questions about this story immediately come to mind. First, why is it newsworthy that a person treats a homeless man with respect rather than disdain? This is remarkable behavior only relative to the background assumption that homeless people are *undeserving* of respect. Second, how does giving the homeless man a US$ 1 token imbue him with dignity? Perhaps this small act of charity by those of us who have something should be welcome by those of us who have nothing. But this relationship of charity does nothing for the dignity of the recipient. Unintentionally, the editors of our local paper demonstrate in the public domain the real need to correct identity-damaging narratives about those who have no place to live and, by extension, those who visit our local food shelf. Los Angeles FEMA local board director, Gene Boutillier, remarks that the "main political task in dealing with poverty is for people to identify with the poor so they can't be demonized and they can't be discounted and they can't be ignored" (as quoted in Poppendieck 1998, 310). The move toward food justice advocacy begins with a good food justice narrative that replaces a damaging story with one that commands respect.

If we identify one *narrative agent* who does something with the food justice narrative, it might be the volunteer. Poppendieck (1998) believes that the entry point to advocacy work is the charity worker who is active in hunger relief programs, since these people are already knowledgeable about who is hungry and are poised to challenge unfairness and address increasing inequalities. There are, of course, national organizations that emphasize public policy work and advocacy as a solution to hunger, such as Bread for the World and the Food Research and Action Center. But many local food shelves, ours included, declare a commitment to social justice as part of their mission. This may be interpreted and acted upon in a number of ways. So it makes sense to enlist the volunteers at the food pantry to show a film, lead a book discussion, or form a local food justice committee to inquire how to initiate policy change as part of rewriting the call to charity. Some of us are teachers and can use already existing food justice narratives or an assignment to write such a story as a way of profiling how hunger is structurally caused and sustained.

Ideally, a food justice narrative should inspire ordinary citizens to undertake individual or collective action on behalf of food justice by shaping our moral imaginations about what is possible. For example, the charity worker may come to see possibilities that depend on existing organizations such as church groups, unions, cooperatives, or food policy councils, and how members can act together to initiate change. In this way an ordinary citizen who works for a charitable organization can become more thoughtfully aware of systemic injustices, if not an activist, in order to discharge her responsibility for justice. The recommendation

I make in this chapter is a practical one. Many writers have identified the need for political and structural change in order to achieve food justice (Allen 2010; Allen and Guthman 2006; Gottlieb and Joshi 2010; Guthman 2008; Hassanein 2003; Sbicca 2012). But if practitioners and ordinary citizens are to be usefully directed to become food justice policy advocates, then we should be prepared to answer *how* they can become advocates. Reading, watching, and reflecting on food justice narratives of the kind I describe here epistemically positions the food shelf volunteer or the charity worker to see what systemic conditions need to change. This is merely one mechanism for achieving what Hassanein (2003) believes is key to transforming the food system—an informed citizenry. In the next chapter we will see why it is also crucial to tell a food justice narrative about who labors in the fields to pick our food.

Garden Journal: Moving Outdoors

In upstate New York spring is a rather drawn out affair and hard to predict. This year to everyone's surprise we had temperatures approaching 80 degrees in March. This was a highly unusual and untrustworthy event since the last frost warning is typically not until Memorial Day. Nonetheless, some garden enthusiasts took the bait. After being cooped up for so many months the thought of planting something outside was just too irresistible, even if a person has to manually thaw part of the soil to do so. Being very impressionable gardeners we moved the cold frame over one of the deep beds, and threw into the partially frozen ground a few short rows of lettuce, spinach, and arugula. "Just as an experiment," Chuck said. By putting it this way we did not invest much in the success or failure of the crop. But the little greens seemed ready for spring as well. We covered them at night by closing the cold frame and let the air circulate when the sun was bright. Not long after we returned to our senses by subsequent cold fronts, rain, sleet, and temperatures approaching 30 degrees, we had an early salad from the March "experiment." In fact, this turned out to be one of the most prolific sections of our garden, supplying us with greens until mid-June.

Meanwhile, the seedlings under the artificial lights in our living room are gaining momentum. At some point, like children, you have to let them go outside to harden off. This is not quite as stressful as raising actual children, but it is time-consuming to introduce trays and trays of young plants to the outside world for a few daylight hours, and then snatch them back indoors in the late afternoon. Gradually they make their way into the cold frame but protected from the sun.

Finally, they are brave and strong enough for us to actually plant them in the newly fluffed deep beds, fortified with compost and horse manure (courtesy of our horse owner friends, Pat and Alan). I imagine our young plants settling into this soil with a sigh of relief after weeks of all the frantic shuffling between temporary homes. The hot pepper trees, flowering and setting fruit by this time, are at last snuggled into container pots of soil. We followed all of John's recommendations regarding these, and expect to see some results.

So now when we lounge on our back deck looking out onto the garden there is something to see. During our morning tour there are green worms to be plucked off broccoli and cabbage plants, cucumber beetles to be snatched from a flower and squished, and there are the rows of bean seedlings to be inspected. Since these are large seeds I am both the planter and guardian of the bean plants—both bush and lima. What is it about these seeds that attract so many birds before they even break the surface of the soil? We did want to create a bird-friendly yard, but there are limits to how friendly I feel when at least half of these bean seeds are taken by flying marauders. After a dismal cucumber harvest last summer I am especially happy with my cucumber plants this year. Patiently, I am directing them to climb the netting attached to our rail fencing. This keeps them off the ground with better air circulation, hopefully minimizing the white mildew fungus that seems to creep into our squash and vine-y vegetables no matter what we do.

Nestled behind the fence where the cucumbers are climbing stand the sunflower sentries. In early spring these volunteers popped up in prohibited areas of the garden, and Chuck threatened to pull them up without the slightest reservation. Admittedly, when we allowed them to grow wherever they wished last year, we ducked and fought our way through these giants by mid-August. So quickly I went to work transplanting the volunteers to a location where they might still add a stately, iconic look to our yard (and be out of the way). They now watch over the crawly, vine-y squash and cucumbers, turning their pretty faces this way and that to follow the sun. Chuck seems a little ruthless now. But in September he will be just as glad to see the chickadees darting in and around these huge seed heads. The sunflowers give us all something to bicker over in a friendly sort of way.

5

Farmworkers: "It is Very Ugly Here"

Three times a day, the bus stops. Two stops a day for food, each time for thirty minutes at a roadside restaurant I would never choose to visit. The restaurants are dirty, with flies all over and a few workers trying frantically to get food for all of us. I begin feeling sick before I even eat the food because of the smells and unsanitary sights. There are two or three choices of food that all entail meat, rice, and soda. Each time, I eat with four of my Triqui companions from San Miguel, including Macario and Joaquin. We take turns buying meals for each other and then eat all together, usually standing up since there isn't enough room to sit. The driver and his assistant are given free meals in exchange for bringing all of us to these restaurants. The conversation during these meals most often revolves around past experiences of violence and suffering on the border. Everyone appears to be on edge, nervous about what might lie ahead. People talk about whether or not we will be caught by the Border Patrol and whether or not we will die trying to cross. (Holmes 2013, 8)

This vivid excerpt by Seth Holmes is from his ethnography, *Fresh Fruit, Broken Bodies: Migrant Farmworkers in the United States* (2013). Here Holmes is describing what it is like to cross the border into the United States as part of a group of Triqui migrant farmworkers from rural Oaxaca State in Mexico. For over a year Holmes undertook to research immigration, social hierarchy and health among the Triqui people from San Miguel, Oaxaca. The methodology he employed was mainly participant observation which, as Holmes puts it, "involves long-term immersion in the everyday lives and practices of people while often including more specific tape-recorded conversations and interviews" (p. 3). The introduction of this ethnography places the reader inside the dangerous and harrowing experience of an illegal border crossing as Holmes is there to testify about each obstacle and how it feels to undertake such a journey.

The stories that Holmes tells about the Triqui and migrant farmworkers, in general, have two sides. The testimony Holmes supplies from the inside makes particular and concrete the way in which the master narrative is damaging. But Holmes also provides the attentive reader with analysis and commentary that shape the basis for a food justice narrative; one that defies ideologies that falsely characterize reasons for labor migration in the first place, and which target and blame the farmworkers themselves for ill health, oppressive working conditions, and poverty. From this exceptional ethnography I explore three features of a damaging master narrative. First, I examine the concept of *voluntary action* as it applies to explanations for why indigenous Mexicans migrate to work in the United States. Second, I scrutinize the presumption that the oppression of farmworkers is morally justified when these oppressions are explained as normal or *natural*. Third, I analyze an underlying assumption about agency that is articulated by some of the subjects that Holmes interviews. This is the idea that *moral agency* is free of constraints, thus implying that individuals (and not social and political conditions) are the appropriate, and sole, loci of moral responsibility and blame. It is worthwhile to explore these three features of the master narrative about US farmworkers since, ultimately, we want to say explicitly how a *food justice narrative* challenges these underlying assumptions and ideologies.

Migration is voluntary

Why do individuals migrate from the Global South to the United States to work in agriculture? Some background assumptions shape the master narrative about labor migration, namely, the distinction between "voluntary, economic, and migrant" and "forced, political, and refugee." Refugees are considered to be candidates for political and social rights in a host country because the explanation for their migration is owed to political conditions that force them to flee their "sending community." But because labor migration is understood to be motivated by economic reasons, it is characterized as voluntary and chosen (Holmes 2013, 17). This is a significant distinction for the following reason. When labor migration is characterized as an individual voluntary choice, the risks and hardships undertaken to cross the border illegally are thought to be risks that are commensurate to the "free" choice to migrate. In this way our collective understanding of the experiences of migrant workers is shaped by the belief that "they can do otherwise" than to advance their economic status by coming to the United States illegally. As Holmes notes, this misrepresents why labor migration occurs by focusing exclusively on individual risky behavior, and contributes to the unjustified ethical conclusion that migrant workers *deserve* their fates and untimely deaths (p. 25). This is part of the damage inflicted on migrant workers by a story that falsely characterizes their migration as voluntary.

Oppression is natural

There are two additional ways in which some master narratives about migrant farmworkers are damaging. One way is by creating a cloak of invisibility that disguises the humanity of the workers themselves and the nature of the oppressions they suffer. Another related way is by morally justifying these oppressions when inequalities are characterized as normal or natural.[1]

The ordinary reader does not know what it is like to subject her body to the kind of abuse that farmworkers endure. Here is how Holmes (2013, 88) introduces us to the embodiment of this kind of work.

> During both of my summers of fieldwork on the Tanaka Brothers Farm, I picked berries once or twice a week and experienced several forms of pain for days afterward. I often felt sick to my stomach the night before picking due to stress about picking the minimum weight. As I picked, my knees continually hurt; I tried different positions, sometimes squatting, sometimes kneeling, sometimes propped up on just one knee. Each time I stood up to take my berries to be weighed, it felt as if a warm liquid like my own blood was running down my pants and into my shoes. All day, I leaned forward to see the strawberries below the leaves, and my neck and back began to hurt by late morning. For two or three days after picking, I took ibuprofen and sometimes used the hot tub in a local private gym to ease the aches, all too aware of the inequality of having access to such amenities.

Two young female pickers described their own experiences. One said that she could no longer feel anything. The other replied that her "knees, back, and hips are always hurting" (Holmes 2013, 89).[2]

On the Tanaka Farm in the Skagit Valley of northwestern Washington, indigenous Oaxacan migrant workers occupy the least desirable position in the labor hierarchy of the farm as contract field workers. This makes them vulnerable to many kinds of unequal treatment. Holmes insists in a charitable way that these conditions are not attributable to selfish or unconcerned farm management (2013, 52). But there is still evidence of what Holmes calls "bad faith" or a collective self-deception about the lives of workers, both on and off the farm. This is evidenced by characterizing "efficient, technical pickers" as "unskilled," or when pickers are barred from English classes, or when the explicit exploitation and mistreatment of workers is hidden or disguised (p. 87).

Here is Marcelina, a twenty-eight-year-old Triqui mother of two, who spoke at a seminar about her experiences picking.

> Good afternoon. I am Marcelina. I come here to the United States to work. A man left me with two children. I wanted to come here to make money, but no. I don't even make enough to send to Oaxaca to my mom who is taking care of my son. Sometimes the strawberry goes poorly, your back hurts, and you don't make anything … It's very difficult here. The farm camp manager doesn't want to give a room to a single woman. So I am living with this family over here [*pointing to a Triqui family of five in the audience*]. One gains nothing here, nothing to survive. Besides that, I have a daughter here with me, and I don't make anything to give her. Working and working. Nothing. I've been here four years and nothing … And then sometimes [the checkers] steal pounds. Sometimes rotten berries make it into the bucket—"Eat that one!" they say, throwing it into your face. They don't work well. And there are hardly any good berries this time of year, pure rotten ones. This is not good. You don't make enough even to eat. I have two children, and it is very ugly here, very ugly to work in the field. That's how it is. Sometimes you want to speak up, but no. You can't speak to them. (Holmes 2013, 75)

This story that Marcelina tells is just a small slice of her life but it points to how she suffers physically as well as psychologically. There is, of course, the poor wages in exchange for backbreaking labor. But as she reports it the assault to her human dignity seems even more offensive. The direct insults by the checkers reveal a basic lack of respect for her as a person.

Samuel echoes these lamentations when he describes his life as a migrant worker in this short interview with Holmes.

> *Samuel:* Here with Tanaka, we don't have to pay rent, but they don't pay us much. They pay 14 cents a pound. And they take out taxes, federal taxes, social security. They pay $20 a day.
>
> … They don't pay fairly. If a person has 34 pounds of strawberries, 4 pounds are stolen because the checker marks only 30. It is not just. That is what bothers people most. People work a lot. They suffer. Humans suffer.
>
> It is easy for them, but for us it is not.
>
> In the blueberries, they steal an ounce from the little boxes and that is why the people can't move ahead. We pick a lot of fruit, and we don't make money.

The people don't say anything. They are afraid of speaking, because the farm will fire them. We want to say things to them, but we can't because we don't have papers. Sometimes the bosses are really mean, and they'll deport you. Sometimes, when one of us says something, they point to the police, and the police can do something to us. That's why people are silent.

Seth: How much do you make each year?

Samuel: One person makes $3,000 to $5,000 a year. We are not asking to be rich. We don't come here to be rich. Yes, it's very little. They say the boss doesn't want us to earn money, and I ask myself, "Why?"

One of Samuel's cousins, Joaquin, testifies to the racial insults he endures:

The supervisors say they'll take away our IDs and fire us if we don't pick the minimum. They tell us we're dropping too many berries, we have to go slow so we don't drop so much. When we go slowly, we don't reach [the minimum] and "Go faster!" They tell us, "You don't know how to work," "Indian, you don't know!" We already know how to work and why the berries drop. If we go slowly, we can't make any money and we get in trouble. If we hurry up, we drop berries and they come and castigate us. "Dumb donkey! "Dog!" We are afraid. (Holmes 2013, 76–7)

All of the workers interviewed give voice to unfair pay and labor practices, insults and racial assaults that violate their human dignity, and physical job-related suffering. But what interferes with the general recognition that these are serious injustices is the idea that their mistreatment and suffering is natural, normal, or deserved (Holmes 2013, 156). The labor hierarchy on the Tanaka Farm illustrates who is targeted for disrespect, who will have little or no access to political power, who will suffer the most egregious ill health, and whose bodies will manifest the worst kinds of painful suffering. Holmes remarks:

The Triqui people inhabit the bottom rung of the pecking order in the Skagit. They live in the coldest and wettest shacks in the most hidden labor camp with no insulation, no heat, and no wooden ceiling under the tin roof. The hold the most stressful, humiliating, and physically strenuous jobs working seven days a week without breaks while exposed to pesticides and weather. Accordingly, the Triqui pickers bear an unequal share of sickness and pain. (p. 96)

When the unequal treatment of the Triqui is *naturalized*, the story told about migrant workers functions to morally justify their social, economic, and political position, thereby depriving them of the opportunity to move into higher wages and less difficult jobs. Holmes interviews Scott, the farm's apple crop manager, and asks why the Triqui are never seen harvesting apples which is the highest paying contract field job.

> He explained, "The O'xacans are too short to reach the apples, they're too slow... They have to use ladders a lot more than some of the other guys. The other guys just use the ladders to pick the very top of the tree, where the O'xacans are having to, you know, halfway ... And, besides, they don't like ladders, anyway."
>
> Ironically, later that week one of Scott's crew bosses told me that her crew's fastest picker was Triqui. Scott continued the above conversation by explaining that O'xacans are perfect for picking berries "because they're lower to the ground." In response to my questions about why Triqui people have different jobs from mestizo Mexicans, several other people state simply, "They're short." The sentiment that Mexicans should pick berries was echoed by U.S. Senator George Murphy from California during a Senate debate on immigration in the 1960s; he stated that Mexicans should be farmworkers because they are "built lower to the ground so it's easier for them to stoop." (Holmes 2013, 171)

Here, the perception of the body naturalizes and thereby justifies the various kinds of injustices experienced by farmworkers.

Individual moral agency

One assumption about agency that emerges from Holmes's ethnography involves blaming individual farmworkers for being poor and holding them responsible for the suffering they endure. As one interviewee says, "You can do anything you want in this country. Anyone can be anything they want to. There is no excuse in this country. There are no barriers. Nothing holds you back except for you. You have no one to blame if you don't become the best you could except for you" (Holmes 2013, 167). This myth about free agency gains whatever plausibility it has from ignoring the contexts that shape constraints on choice, action, and opportunity. Consider, for example, how this "a contextual" assumption about agency interferes with the basic need to be healthy.

When the Triqui find themselves in need of healthcare they are at the mercy of overt racism, hurried diagnoses by overburdened health care practitioners, and sometimes an indifferent or even a willful misunderstanding of their culture and their lives as migrant workers. The ethically salient feature here is that whatever ails the Triqui is explained by their *individual* behavior; the "choice" they make to work in the fields, or their individual failings to keep themselves and their families healthy. In this sense health professionals fail to recognize that there are more fundamental causes of their patients' suffering that make reference to social, economic, and political structures. This is so despite the evidence of a great deal of compassion for patients and a sense of calling to contribute to better health of migrant workers. Holmes remarks, "Physicians in the United States and Mexico are not trained to see the social determinants of health problems, or to hear them when communicated by their patients" (2013, 152). For example, clinicians may blame the sickness on the patient when she is charged with an inappropriate diet, or when she assumes the incorrect way of bending when picking berries. In this way treatments, or failures to treat health problems of workers, "depoliticizes suffering" as well as reinforces the oppressions that produce sickness in the first place.[3] As Holmes says, "The contemporary bio behavioral clinical gaze must be transformed to recognize the social, political, and economic determinants of sickness and health" (p. 154). When individual agency is stripped of context that explains how "choices" about work, health, housing, and education are constrained by fundamental structural conditions, then it is easier to morally blame farmworkers themselves for failing to improve their lives. But this account of agency is misleading. When combined with stories implying that labor migration is voluntary, and the naturalizing of unjust hierarchies, we have all of the ingredients of an oppressive master narrative that can and should be challenged.

Case study: *Fresh Fruit, Broken Bodies*

Holmes's immersion methodology allows the reader to see up-close what it is like to work in the fields, manage ill health, live in poor housing conditions, and to constantly negotiate the marginalization and exploitation suffered by US migrant farmworkers. The reader gets to know his research subjects, really his friends and companions, who share their lives and experiences. This kind of inside testimony is ideal for constructing a food justice narrative. When Holmes describes the experiences of crossing the border, living in substandard housing, the bodily damage suffered from fieldwork, and the constant moving from one harvest to the next, he creates a story that is particular to concrete places and the people who inhabit them. These are people he knows and cares about. These are good people who work hard under insufferable conditions for little pay.

Holmes, the narrator, also speaks to us from the *outside*—explaining, classifying, and analyzing the oppressions and injustices that farmworkers experience. Holmes points to the unjust circumstances of their lives and passionately expresses his moral indignation. This external perspective is the ethical conclusion that the reader is invited to share. The three features of a food justice narrative (particularity, emotional engagement, and accuracy) are doing significant explanatory work in this extraordinary ethnography. Seen as a food justice narrative, *Fresh Fruit, Broken Bodies* effectively defies the damaging stories about migrant workers we have identified above; namely, that migration is voluntary, oppression is natural, and that individual agency operates everywhere freely of constraints.

Consider how we learn about the inequalities of treatment in the day to day living of migrant workers. When Holmes accompanies a Triqui family to Burger King for dinner on payday, his friends are not given the right amount of food for their order. Holmes (2013, 36) suggests casually that someone should go ask at the counter for the rest of the order.

> Samuel and his wife, Leticia, looked at each other with furrowed brows. They explained to me that they could never do such a thing because they would not be given different fries and would likely get in trouble for asking. Samuel told me to go up to see what they would do to a *gabacho*. As I expected, they gave us four large fries and apologized kindly-resentfully. Samuel was amazed. My body was treated as though it had and deserved power, whereas theirs have been treated repeatedly as underlings, undeserving of respect.

Again and again Holmes is privy to inequalities of treatment where his Triqui companions are charged the wrong amounts, given the wrong medicines, and treated as inferiors. They carefully and fearfully negotiate police officers when traveling, keeping their vehicles in perfect shape so that they will not be pulled over. This particularity of experience positions the reader to feel what it is like to occupy a position at the lowest rung of a social and economic hierarchy. As Holmes remarks, "After many months of living, eating, seeking medical treatment, and driving with migrant workers in the United States, it became clear that everyone around us recognized my body as belonging in a significantly different place in our society's power structure than did the bodies of my Triqui friends" (2013, 37). What is achieved by Holmes's attention to particularity of place and people is that he makes visible the humanity of migrant workers. In this way the reader comes to share the narrator's point of view that depicts migrant workers as "fellow humans, skilled and hard workers, people treated unfairly with the odds against them" (p. 29).

We see Holmes's own emotional reading of these events and circumstances but also the emotional lives of his companions from their own point of view; the Triqui families that invite him into their homes. These emotions are educative for the reader by guiding her affective responses to the events described including fear, aspirations and hopes, and moral indignation. Consider, for example, this emotionally charged excerpt about the border crossing.

> After we have hiked through blisters for many miles and I have shared all my ibuprofen with the others, we stop to rest in a large, dry creek bed under the cover of several trees. We fall asleep, using torn-open plastic trash bags as blankets. Our coyote leaves to talk with his contact on a nearby Native American reservation about giving us a ride past the second border checkpoint to Phoenix. He returns, anxious, telling us his contact no longer gives rides because of the increased Border Patrol activity. We discuss pooling our money and buying a car to drive ourselves or looking for someone else to drive us. Two of the men try to convince me to drive them into Phoenix, past the internal Border Patrol checkpoints. I tell them that would be a felony and would mean I would go to prison and lose the ability to work. They seemed satisfied by my response, respecting the need to be able to work. After we decide to look for another ride, our coyote sneaks off to look for a different driver. We wait for a few hours. We rest quietly, drink Gatorade, and brush our teeth in the creek bed.
>
> Suddenly, our coyote runs back speaking quickly in Triqui. Two Border Patrol agents—one black and one white—appear running through the trees, jump down into our creek bed, and point guns at us. (Holmes 2013, 20–21)

Holmes does not need to add to this report, "And we felt afraid." The reader is tensely following the events as if she were there. And when the group is caught by Border Patrol the reader is not indifferent, bored, or remotely analytical about this event. Our fears and sympathies are already engaged by the circumstances as told from the inside, as a traveler who is risking everything to cross the border.[4]

When Marcelina tells us that "It is very ugly here. It is very ugly in the fields," we feel the anger and frustration that she voices. It will do no good to complain because most of the pickers are vulnerable as undocumented workers. They will not risk losing their jobs and possibly being deported. So Marcelina's moral indignation becomes ours as we hear what it is like from her point of view, knowing these conditions are unfair but seeing that she is powerless to effect change. The reader's affective responses to the individual stories told by Holmes and his Triqui companions is a crucial feature of this food justice narrative. Once we see the larger contextual circumstances that constrain choices and create psychological and physical suffering, our feeling of compassion triggers the judgment that these events are unjust.

Part of understanding the plight of migrant farmworkers in a food justice narrative involves getting the facts right.[5] In this case "accuracy" means clarifying why migrant workers are here in the first place. Our agriculture requires cheap labor, but political policies and laws make entering our country illegal. This means that migrant farmworkers have no way to influence those laws or institutions that extract the maximum amount of labor for minimal protections in pay, health care, education, or social services (Holmes 2013, 13). The idea that labor migration is voluntary and chosen is false. The Triqui companions say to Holmes that they are forced to migrate in order to survive. Macario says at one point to Holmes, "There is no other option left for us" (pp. 17–18). The Triqui who do attempt border crossings say that it is riskier to attempt to live in their host country in San Miguel without access to "work, money, food, or healthcare" (p. 21).

Perhaps the clearest way of thinking about how the concept of force operates here is by comparison to the cases about "smuggled" or trafficked sex workers discussed in Chapter 3. Recall that Meyers (2016, 40) is concerned to establish that these women are victims of human rights abuse even though they are not classified in this way under any standard victim paradigms. As part of her analysis Meyers recommends that we use and apply the norms of force, fraud, and coercion to explain why these migrants "choose" to accept what they believe to be legal jobs abroad. For example, Meyers uses the concept of *force* to capture conditions of poverty that produce only a few desperate options for trafficked sex workers. Likewise, there is a similar story about labor migration that challenges the idea that migrant workers freely choose to enter the United States illegally to work in the fields. Here is how Abelino, a thirty-five-year-old father of four, describes why the Triqui people have to leave their homes in Mexico.

> In Oaxaca, there's no work for us. There's no work. There's nothing. When there's no money, you don't know what to do. And shoes, you can't get any. A shoe like this [*pointing to his tennis shoes*] costs about 300 Mexican pesos. You have to work two weeks to buy a pair of shoes. A pair of pants costs 300. It's difficult. We come here and it is a little better, but you still suffer in the work. Moving to another place is also difficult. Coming here with the family and moving around to different places, we suffer. The children miss their classes and don't learn well. Because of this, we want to stay here only for a season with [legal immigration] permission and let the children study in Mexico. Do we have to migrate to survive? Yes, we do. (Holmes 2013, 91)

Conditions of survival force individuals and groups to undertake the risks involved in migration. But we will not see this reality unless we profile those background conditions that constrain and limit "choices" as part of a food justice narrative. These background conditions include larger social and economic circumstances that directly influence the Triqui's ability to survive in their own country. "In order to survive, Triqui people are forced to leave their homes, cross a potentially fatal border, and work in an inhospitable environment. The economic and political conditions forcing them to migrate are caused directly by international policies and military actions that lead to global, regional, and local inequalities and suffering" (Holmes 2013, 188). Part of the problem in seeing that labor migration is not voluntary or chosen is that the focus remains on the behavior of the individual person. What is missing from such an account is reference to the systemic conditions that create economic hardship for populations and groups. Here is how Holmes supplies the larger structural context surrounding labor migration.

> Especially important is the U.S.-initiated North American Free Trade Agreement (NAFTA) banning economic barriers, including tariffs, between signatory countries. Thus, the Mexican government was forced to erase tariffs, including that on corn, the primary crop produced by indigenous families in southern Mexico. However, NAFTA and other free trade policies do not ban government subsidies. Thus the U.S. government was allowed to increase corn subsidies year after year, effectively enacting an inverse tariff against Mexican corn. In addition, such subsidies are only possible for relatively wealthy countries and could not be enacted by the relatively poor Mexican government. During my fieldwork in San Miguel, I watched genetically engineered corporately grown corn from the U.S. Midwest underselling local, family-grown corn in the same village. (p. 25)

Holmes is well aware that the story about labor migration needs retelling. This revised narrative will describe the facts about migrant workers in a particular way. It will not localize risk and blame around individual people. Rather, it will explain those structural forces that create vulnerable populations, depriving them of opportunities to work, feed themselves and their families, get an education, and live healthy lives. By profiling those conditions that create labor migration in the first place, such as NAFTA and the Central American Free Trade Agreement, we are better able to identify what structural conditions need to change, as opposed to the individual behavior of those who are directly affected by these external conditions (Holmes 2013, 26).

Holmes's ethnography qualifies as a food justice narrative because it resists a damaging master narrative about migrant farmworkers by correcting false assumptions and inaccuracies. This is achieved in a unique way by inviting the reader inside the story to experience what it is like to illegally cross the US border, labor in the fields, be treated unequally, and be racially insulted. This creates a narrative rich with the *particularity* of place and persons. It also supplies the reader with numerous opportunities to engage her *emotions* by feeling with the characters Holmes knows and writes about. Fear, moral indignation, and compassion are some of the appropriate affective responses to the story we are reading. These responses also signal how to *construe* the circumstances that unequally position the Triqui and other migrant farmworkers. According to Holmes, the kinds of injustices experienced by undocumented migrant workers is not intended by malicious corporate executives, farm managers, or owners. It is produced and sustained by larger structures, and realized in a variety of ways in the economic and social lives of workers (Holmes 2013, 31). When we directly witness Samuel's indignation about unfair labor practices and low pay for the hard work done, our feelings of indignation guide our moral judgment that this is a case of exploitation. Iris Marion Young (1990, 49–50) characterizes one "face" of oppression as *exploitation*, describing this as "a steady process of the transfer of the results of the labor of one social group to benefit another," including social rules about what work is done, for whom, and how it is compensated. Marcelina voices her despair that insults and disrespectful treatment cannot be addressed from fear of retaliation about the loss of employment and possible deportation. Her situation is one of *powerlessness*. Young describes this "face" of oppression as a division of social class between professionals and nonprofessionals that divides not just the kind of labor assigned, but a difference of power relations between social groups. As Young says, "The powerless are those who lack authority … situated so that they must take orders and rarely have the right to give them … and who have little or no autonomy … and do not command respect" (pp. 56–7). When Holmes maintains that readers and theoreticians need to "denaturalize social inequalities," he understands first that we need to see these inequalities in the particular lives of those who are affected. Part of the transformation for the reader of *Fresh Fruit, Broken Bodies* is to learn to *see* how these social inequalities are realized because, to a large extent, the oppressions suffered by migrant farm workers are invisible (p. 185).

Ideally a food justice narrative positions the reader to identify what can and should change as a matter of justice. The last chapter of Holmes's ethnography includes practical recommendations for improving the lives of farmworkers. For example, he urges solidarity in order to defeat local, federal, and international policies that contribute to inequality and injustice for migrant farmworkers. These activist objectives include, for example, buying and promoting food from farms that treat workers fairly, lobbying for more humane immigration policies, and petitioning for better access to education and healthcare for workers. Many of these same themes that inspire activism on behalf of migrant farmworkers are also on display in the documentary film, *Food Chains: The Revolution in America's Fields* (Longoria and Schlosser 2014).

Case study: *Food Chains*

This dramatic story follows the Coalition of Immokalee Workers (CIW) and their supporters as they stage a six-day hunger strike in front of the Publix corporate headquarters in Immokalee, Florida. Publix is a grocery store chain that dominates the landscape in Florida with more than 700 outlets. The CIW is gathered here to pressure executives from the corporation to meet with farmworkers in order to discuss signing onto the Fair Food Program (n.d. *Coalition of Immokalee Workers*). This program involves a code of conduct to protect farmworkers against human rights violations in the field, as well as a pledge to pay a penny more per pound for tomatoes to go directly to farmworker wages. The CIW has tried every other way to get Publix to sit for a meeting about the Fair Food Program but, so far, Publix has refused to acknowledge the workers at the bottom of the tomato food chain. This riveting story about activism on behalf of migrant workers makes for an ideal food justice narrative whose target audience is the general public as well as students and scholars. As with other case studies discussed here, I profile the three main features of a food justice narrative on display: particularity, the education of our emotions, and accuracy conditions.

The captivating style of this film allows the viewer to hear directly from the tomato workers about what their lives are like. There is no obvious mediating presence, like an interviewer, to distract our attention from their faces, their earnest desire to live well, their voices that sometimes express resignation, sometimes hope, but also moral indignation. We see in the opening scene a family that is transporting a young child from bed to babysitter in the darkness at 5:00 A.M. so that the husband and wife can board the bus to the fields to begin their day picking tomatoes. Scenes from the field show workers engaged in quick, repetitive nonstop picking, running to keep up, and heaving baskets of tomatoes up in the air to be dumped and loaded onto a truck. These are stark reminders about the texture of this particular kind of life. And from the workers themselves we understand what matters. It is not just that the work is hard; this is something that is acceptable. Rather, it is the insult to integrity when it is clear "how little you mean to the people you work for." The details that create a compelling food justice narrative are those that allow us to see the particular circumstances of living from the point of view of the workers themselves. And what we see is the resolve to be visible and to disclose their common humanity. Some of the farmworkers who participate in the hunger strike wear placards that say, "I am human too." As if we need reminding.

The issues profiled in the film echo the same forms of oppression discussed in Holmes's ethnography. We see how *exploitation* is realized by learning that tomato workers earn approximately $42.00 working in the fields for 10–12 hours, exposed to sun, heat, and pesticide drift. The amount earned per year is between $10,000 and $13,000, and barely covers food and shelter, let alone health care, emergency medical treatment, and childcare.[6] A new instance of *powerlessness* is revealed when we learn that roughly 80 percent of women who do field work have experienced some kind of sexual abuse or harassment. But these women are not in a position to complain because they risk either losing their jobs, or being deported if they are undocumented. Either outcome is frightening since the women who are subject to sexual harassment and abuse are poor. They are supporting children and extended family and will be entirely destitute without any employment whatsoever. Their situation is similar to the Triqui migrant workers in Holmes's ethnography who quietly lament unfair labor practices (e.g., not weighing berries accurately). The economic vulnerability of women in the tomato industry who have been sexually harassed creates desperate and few options. These women may *feel* powerless in the face of their plight but powerlessness is essentially a state of affairs in the world.[7] The concept captures what most migrant farmworkers experience; unfair economic conditions, assaults on their dignity as human beings, and lack of respect without *opportunities for redress*. This last feature is crucial for understanding what it means to be powerless. Because there is little governmental oversight to enforce already existing laws designed to protect against sexual abuse and harassment, the voices of women who experience this abuse are "disabled."

The viewer of the film *Food Chains* is a daily witness to the hunger strike outside of the Publix corporate office. It is almost as if we too are waiting for something to happen; even some small token of recognition from Publix about the very visible presence of farmworkers gathered in plain sight of the executive offices. What we do hear is the disembodied voice of a Publix spokesperson who claims that the corporation does not get involved in labor disputes, and reminding the public that Publix has a reputation for charitable donations to the community. This appeal to charity echoes some of our earlier themes in Chapters 3 and 4 about solutions to food insecurity. Publix may believe that charitable donations absolve them of responsibility for the lamentable economic conditions of tomato pickers who harvest the tomatoes they sell in their grocery stores. But the narrator of the film does not let this claim go unchallenged. Rather, the exploitation of tomato pickers is explained by reference to larger and more complicated conditions about food supply chains. We learn that only a few mega corporations, like Publix, control the prices for foods purchased from suppliers and farmers. The prices set by these large corporations are not negotiable by those suppliers who want to sell their food. In order to meet these very low purchase prices suppliers must cut their costs elsewhere, to the farmer and, ultimately, all the way down the food chain to the workers themselves. These are the larger structural conditions that most of us fail to see unless these conditions are explicitly made part of the story about food justice. The economic pressure to meet the purchase price set by Publix and other large corporate buyers is also felt by the farmers or owners of the fields who hire migrant workers. The film allows us to see constrained choices here as well. But these constraints are depicted less sympathetically when compared with fieldworkers who make less than minimum wage. Remember that Holmes echoes the same explanation about these systemic conditions when he cautions against the temptation to vilify the owners of the Tanaka farm. He reminds us that the owners of the farm are also at the mercy of the economy and market prices determined by other factors which are out of their control. The food supply chain story identifies corporations, like Publix, as entities with power and economic influence. Moreover, the story implicates these corporations with the moral responsibility to address migrant workers' exploitation that trickles down from price setting at the top. The film is effective in meeting the accuracy conditions of a food justice narrative because it realistically construes the conditions of migrant farm labor as creating kinds of oppression; namely, economic exploitation and powerlessness. Satisfying these accuracy conditions is achieved by making visible the humanity of the workers themselves, but also by disclosing the contexts of the food supply chains that explain *why* farmworkers are exploited and powerless. Targeting Publix as an agent of change to correct these conditions seems exactly appropriate, if only they would acknowledge the farmworkers.

Perhaps the most emotionally moving part of this story is inspired by those who participate in the hunger strike itself. The viewer is directly and intimately acquainted with how the farmworkers and their supporters are feeling from one day to the next. Their initial hopefulness and spirited beginning to the strike gradually dissipates as the week drags on. We see not only the physical toll taken as they continue to go without food, but also the strikers' despair and resignation about the failure to trigger any response by Publix whatsoever. One spokesperson for the CIW remarks that while Publix has many millions of dollars to devote to advertising their position, we have our *bodies* to tell the message. But the bodies of farmworkers themselves are not enough to bring Publix to the table this time. We might predict that the immediate failure of the hunger strike would create hopelessness in the strikers. But artfully the story of this particular strike is juxtaposed against the historical newsreel of Cesar Chavez, who in 1968 undertook a month-long hunger strike on behalf of approximately 100,000 farmworkers—members and supporters of the United Farmworkers Union in the Central Valley of California.[8] The particular poignant scene revisited in *Food Chains* shows President Robert Kennedy breaking the fast with Chavez, sharing bread and his support for farmworkers. As one member of the CIW says, "[farmworkers] have a long tradition of creative non-violence. And what this achieves is to bring out the character of your opposition." The character of Publix is on clear display. But what this particular glance backwards contextualizes is the long view of the struggle taking place in front of the Publix Corporate Headquarters. Instead of despair there is a strong spirit of camaraderie among those who end their hunger strike by marching three miles to break bread with friends and supporters. This moment in the film is riveting. Even though we have been "present" throughout each day of the strike, we take our emotional cues about optimism and hope from those who are looking ahead to the next stage of the fight for fair food.

Conclusion

Fresh Fruit, Broken Bodies and *Food Chains* are two exceptional food justice narratives. They each illustrate how best to profile particularity of place and people, how best to use the characters' stories to educate our emotions, and how to morally construe the circumstances of farmworkers' lives to reveal oppressive and exploitative conditions that deprive these workers of the opportunity to live well. Each narrative guides the attentive reader to more complex structural background conditions that create and sustain food injustice. These background conditions include: free trade agreements, immigration policy, unfair labor practices, the role of large corporations in the food chain, and insufficient regulatory oversight to protect women in the fields from sexual harassment and abuse (to name just a few). A food justice narrative should do exactly this kind of explanatory work by making visible to the reader or viewer these injustices as part of the accurate story about migrant farmworkers. In this way a food justice narrative does more than inspire sympathy and compassion for the individuals who labor to pick our food. It focuses the lens of moral indignation on public policy, laws, institutions, and political ideology. These are the more fundamental conditions that can and should change if we are truly interested in justice for migrant farmworkers.[9]

The extended case studies discussed here also echo a theme from earlier chapters about food insecurity. Specifically, food justice narratives about farmworkers defy an explanation of injustice attributable to individual choices, for example, the "choice" to illegally cross the border into the United States to work in the fields. Likewise in Chapters 3 and 4 we rejected damaging master narratives that explained hunger and food insecurity by reference to individual behavior and circumstances of living that included accidental misfortune and tragedy specific to individual women and communities in need. In the next chapter seeing what matters ethically requires renewed focus on the background conditions that situate individuals who suffer from the condition of obesity. In these cases adjusting the ethical lens involves rewriting the story about individual moral responsibility in order to explain who is obese and why.

Garden Journal: Too Much Kale

Once most of our seedlings are settled into the raised beds, there is still a bit of frantic activity to support them. I always make sure they are watered well enough right at the start. The last thing a gardener wants to see is a severe droopy reaction in a new transplant. Now we are looking out at a monster garden. Everywhere tall green giants shoot up from the beds. The sunflowers are spectacular, standing six feet tall—clearly the alpha plant. But my eye catches on the roses also. This year our climbing rose is a knockout. It crawls up the cedar arbor Chuck created over one of our pebble paths displaying bright red roses blanketing the arbor beginning low near the ground, solidly rising to the top, and draping over on three sides. This rose receives very little attention from us. It just seems to do its thing better and better each year. I have been fond of this plant since I planted it three years ago in the middle of the summer. I boldly announced that it would reach the top of the arbor by the end of its first growing season. Chuck scoffed. "I don't think so," he said with too much skepticism for me to let go. "Okay, I'll bet you a nice dinner that it will get that high." Of course, I won that bet when the rose crawled to the top and reached several feet higher by September.

By now we are harvesting and eating kale, rainbow chard, lettuce, young onions, cucumbers, and a variety of herbs: parsley, cilantro, basil (!), and oregano. Our experimental fennel crop is fluffy and fern-like on top. We do not really know what is underneath because we have never grown this, but we cannot wait to find out. Part of the fun is figuring out what to do with fennel (or any new vegetable or herb a novice gardener tries for the first time). Once a gardener plants a seed, nourishes a young plant, and successfully harvests the produce, she has something considerable invested in the outcome … eating it. So the least we can do is to look around for recipes and cooking advice for this new addition to our harvest. I will let you know how that goes in the case of fennel. I do not even know what this is really—a bulb, an herb, a root vegetable?

One grand success this year is the garlic. Chuck used some of our own bulbs from last year's harvest, planting twice as many cloves as in previous years. When these go into the ground in late fall and are buried in leaves and compost, it is really hard to believe that they will be the first green things we see rising out of the bed. Now, in July, we have snipped the curly garlic scapes, and a few weeks later pulled the huge bulbs from the soil to let them dry on a wire screen supported over the top of the raised bed. They are now hanging upside down in our garage, suspended from parallel wires on a beam strung above the snow blower. Both the garlic and the snow blower are bidding their time, waiting to assist us.

It is late summer in the North Country, and we are all hot, hot, hot. There is no getting around watering our vegetables (and perennials), though we have let the various ground covers turn brown, including the lawn. But wow! What a display we have now. The tomatoes especially are enjoying a banner year, each plant setting more fruit than it can support. We have propped, tied, trimmed, and finally just let them sag with the weight of twenty lbs. of tomatoes hanging off of their slender stalks. What is more thrilling is that the plants show no sign of late blight, a deadly murdering fungus that attacked the entire tomato crop in our part of the country two years ago. These fruits are perfectly shaped, barely showing a blushing pink. And now it is clear that we have too many of these plants. Maybe we are still miffed about our less than healthy tomato harvest last year? Somehow this has influenced our decision in the early spring to plant six more additional plum tomato plants (for canning). But now I am wondering if this was just too ambitious!

And, we cannot seem to keep up with the lively growth of purple kale and rainbow chard. Since we now like to eat these leafy greens, we allowed five or six plants to mature from seedlings, and they all survived. Obviously this was too much hubris as well. I have cut leaves for my friends Deb and Loni, but I have decided I need a more systematic kale and chard removal system. This was the rationale for visiting the Senior Center to ask the Director, Patti, if the kitchen might be able to use these extra vegetables. Apparently not unless I can bring enough for 700 meals distributed to seniors across the North Country. This was a bit more food than I could contract for ... at least right now. But some of the seniors gather for Bingo, lunch, and conversation. The biggest attendance day is Thursday. So Patti agreed that I should bring some bags of produce, whatever I have, and let the visiting seniors take what they want back to their own homes.

So this is what I have done for four consecutive Thursdays. At first I believed that I should contribute my vegetables to a food shelf, and there is one in our town that accepts fresh food. Since I only have to walk two blocks from my house to the Senior Center, I wondered—am I doing the easy thing or the right thing with the extra beans, tomatoes, kale, and chard? But as I chat with some of my "clients" at the Senior Center I realize that while this may be a population of people who can afford fresh food, they still have limited access to it. This is because there are mobility obstacles. Some seniors live in housing near the Center; others arrive for meals and social events by bus. It is pretty obvious that many of them will not show up to shop for fresh vegetables at the farmer's market in town. It is just too hard to get there for a person who does not drive or who uses a walker for transportation. And my conversations here reveal a kind of nostalgia for growing food. One older woman shuffled across the room as I unpacked the few vegetables that I had managed to bring that week. When she arrived at the table she told me how much she loved chard! Really? I must have sounded surprised because it is my least favorite of the leafy greens. "Oh yes." She proceeded to reminisce about her own garden, long since relinquished but not forgotten. I happily packed her a bag of large green leaves with bright red stems, and threw in a few ripe tomatoes. I feel like I am on the edge of something here—an on-site farmer's market. But to make this happen I will either have to start raiding other gardens for more produce, or plan to grow more rows of vegetables next year.

6

Obesity, Responsibility, and Situated Agency

"There is almost no accounting for personal responsibility. People should be (and I believe they are) capable of not consuming everything the market throws their way" (as quoted in Guthman 2011, 50). This quote invites us to take a closer look at what personal responsibility means in connection to the "problem" of obesity and recommended solutions.[1] What we find in obesity discourse is that the language of personal responsibility sometimes has a moral dimension to it, although the attribution of moral responsibility rarely comes equipped with any clear criteria of application. This is true across a wide range of settings where the expression "personal responsibility" is employed by academics, policy analysts, representatives of the food industry, or by ordinary citizens. Thus there is an urgent need to clarify the concept of moral responsibility and how it applies in these contexts. I argue that a food justice narrative makes visible how exemption conditions operate by attention to the particular lived experience of being obese. A food justice narrative positions us to make more accurate and nuanced appraisals of moral responsibility about individual people who struggle with the problem of obesity.

Another reason for demanding clarity about the concept of moral responsibility as it applies to obesity discourse is that we may be able to use such an account to resist a false dichotomy about moral agency.[2] A prevalent idea about responsibility and obesity seems to suggest one of two possibilities. Either individuals are unequivocally responsible for their condition of being obese. Or individuals are excused from moral accountability because their condition of obesity is owed primarily to external conditions; namely, the "toxic" food environment, social institutions, public policy, the corporate food industry, or more fundamental unjust structural conditions (Brownell and Horgen 2004; Brownell et al. 2010; Nestle 2002, 2015). As an example of the first position, when defenders of freedom of choice resist the regulation of processed foods and foods high in salt, sugar, and fat, they assume a much too expansive and liberal account of moral agency. They suppose (or want to convince us) that individual consumers already enjoy complete knowledge about the health dangers of processed food, and that they have an ideal kind of freedom to choose what to eat and how much to eat.[3] However, as I argue, it is more realistic to suppose that moral agents are actually embedded in situations that, to a greater or lesser degree, constrain their knowledge of ethically salient features of the world and constrain the amount of control they have over their actions (Brownell and Warner 2009). Alternatively, when environmental features of the world are implicated as part of a causal explanation for obesity we are better able to focus on those social and political background conditions that disadvantage populations of people (Guthman 2011; Kirkland 2011). These contexts, to a greater or lesser degree, limit a person's access to knowledge and create obstacles to eating healthy food. But by exclusively emphasizing these external conditions it is easy to lose sight of the agency of individual people; what they know and how they can choose to act within the spheres of opportunity open to them. To capture this more realistic idea we should try to formulate a precise way of describing the kind of *situated* moral agency of individuals that continues to operate even in circumstances that constrain choices and limit opportunities.[4]

Finding moral fault

In ordinary discourse about obesity and personal responsibility we can detect a moral complaint about those who are obese and how they came to be that way. Consider the following student comments as reported by Guthman (2011, 50–51):

> I think the people who eat the fast food are to blame. It is *their* choice to pull up to the drive-through, or to "supersize" their meal … Although I agree that advertising and the food industry is partly at fault for advertising snack foods, I still feel that it is ultimately an individual choice to eat these foods. It basically comes down to will power. There are always temptations in life, but that doesn't mean we have to go after those temptations.

In this context what *personal responsibility* means is not merely that an obese person is the proximate cause of her condition, but that she bears some moral responsibility for those actions that lead to being obese. A related moral criticism takes the form of impugning the obese person's moral character as intemperate (excessive in appetitive desires), lacking in self-discipline, or lazy. On this view it might be thought that individuals who are obese are morally responsible for their condition because they have not tried hard enough, or simply have not opted to live in a healthy way. One of Guthman's students articulates the concern this way:

> I believe in this day and age, people know exactly what they are eating … My argument is that people do know, many times they simply choose not to live healthy lifestyles, and *this* is the major cause of obesity." (Guthman 2011, 50–51)

On this view of things choosing not to improve oneself or choosing not to live a healthy lifestyle are reasons to morally fault the character of an individual person for poor decision-making and actions over a long period of time. Here I call this kind of explanation about obese individuals the "moral fault [master] narrative." This kind of story is echoed in the popular media as well. A recent issue of *Parade* magazine was devoted to the popular TV reality show, *The Biggest Loser* (Ashton 2016). In the accompanying article this year's trainers (Jen, Bob, and Dolvett) recommend various ways to lose weight by resisting temptation. Some of these "temptation busters" include identifying and avoiding triggers to overeating, stocking your kitchen with only healthy foods, creating small exercise goals, and working out with a friend for extra motivation. There is nothing surprising here. In fact, these recommendations capture a very plausible intuition; *we* are in charge of our health. And if we just try hard enough, then we might be more successful in losing weight or adopting a healthier lifestyle. However, the flip side of the temptation busters' recommendations is that if the weight does not come off, surely it is because the obese agent did not try hard enough to resist these temptations. What I challenge about the moral fault narrative is the implication that the locus of moral responsibility rests entirely on the person who is obese in isolation from the circumstances that affect her food choices.[5] At the same time, it is still true that the population of obese individuals are moral agents whose *general* capacities are intact for making free and informed choices. Nothing I will say about situated agency directly contradicts this very plausible idea.

Perhaps the ideal target of these moral criticisms about unhealthy eating is a person I call "Alex." Alex is determined to adopt a healthier lifestyle. She believes that she can do so by limiting her consumption of salty, sugary, and fatty foods, exercising more by riding her bike, walking to work, and by attending a weekly Zumba class at the gym where she is a member. As part of her research about nutrition, Alex learns that a twelve-ounce can of Coke or Pepsi contains nine teaspoons of sugar (Nestle 2015). Because of this bit of knowledge she comes to believe that soda is not part of a healthy diet. She forms the intention to avoid buying and consuming soda despite her desire to do so. Nonetheless, on a particular occasion in context *C1* Alex is out to lunch with her friends at Applebee's and she orders a Coke to go with her salad. Is Alex morally responsible for this action in context *C1*? Applying a particular theory of responsibility to this *basic* illustrative example about Alex can help us see how to answer this question more precisely.

Responsibility and volitional control

To make some progress on the moral issues connected to obesity, I employ a particular theory of moral responsibility formulated by Manuel Vargas (2013a, 2013b) in order to explain what it means to say that an individual is morally responsible for being obese (or not). Vargas holds what he calls a "revisionist reasons" account of moral responsibility.[6] What is central to *reasons* accounts, in general, is that in order for a moral agent to be morally responsible for an action she performs, she must have the capacity to respond to reasons.[7] First, she must be capable of having the relevant kind of *knowledge* about herself and the world to recognize good reasons for acting. Second, she must be capable of responding to reasons by exerting the relevant kind of freedom and *control* over her actions. In other words, the agent must have the capacity to translate these reasons into motivations for acting, and successfully perform an action based on these reasons. I will not argue for Vargas's theory, per se, but I believe that it is independently plausible and, furthermore, possesses suitable resources for addressing the complexity of the case study of obesity.[8] This is so because it allows us to include in our assessment of individual responsibility those particular features of the environment that are relevant to an individual's knowledge about and control over what she eats. This kind of situated agency is important for preserving our intuitions about how and why people act in practical and real-world settings.

What is interestingly different about Vargas's account compared to other reasons accounts of responsibility is that moral agents are judged responsible or not based on satisfying the knowledge and control conditions in a particular set of circumstances, *C*. By adopting what he calls "circumstantialism" about capacities, Vargas thus rejects some standard assumptions that characterize other accounts of responsibility. One is the idea that agents are the kinds of beings that have free will because they have an intrinsic feature or property like a *real self*, or rationality, either of which may be characterized as a "cross-situationally stable mechanism" specifiable in isolation from the agent's external social or physical environment. These more standard assumptions about responsibility typically imply, for example, that both infants and schizophrenics are exempt from responsibility because they lack this global and intrinsic ability to reason.[9] Instead Vargas recommends that we conceive of responsible agency as a local and context-sensitive capacity that is realized (or not) in actual or possible situations. In other words, our rational capacities and our capacities for self-governance are not enjoyed independently of circumstances and situations, but are contingent on these circumstances.[10]

Vargas formulates the conditions for responsible agency by capturing a basic intuition. In order to be morally responsible for an action agents must be capable of knowing and understanding morally relevant reasons for acting (detection), and they must also be capable of successfully acting on these moral reasons by exhibiting self-governance (volitional control).[11] These two conditions are further explained by specifying that the capacities for detection and volitional control may be realized in the agent's actual circumstances *or* in other possible circumstances that are "relevantly similar" to the actual circumstances (Vargas 2013a, 214).

In order to illustrate how to use and apply Vargas's two conditions for being morally responsible for an action, let's return to hypothetical Alex in our basic example. Is Alex morally responsible for her action in context *C1*—consuming the Coke? Alex appears to be capable of detecting the moral considerations that are relevant to her action of consuming the Coke in *C1*. These considerations likely include Alex's intention to adopt a healthier lifestyle, her belief that eating nutritional food contributes to that goal, the particular knowledge Alex has about the sugar content in soda, and her belief that she ought to avoid drinking soda if she wants to lose weight and to live a healthier lifestyle[12]. But does Alex also have the capacity for volitional control in this context? Let us suppose that Alex is sufficiently aware of these moral considerations at the time she is ordering lunch, and let us suppose that she is motivated to pursue a course of action that these moral considerations favor. Nonetheless, in spite of this she buys and consumes the sugary beverage. Now we should try to determine whether or not this action is merely a lack of willpower for which we can hold her morally responsible. In other words, does Alex have the *capacity* for volitional control in this context? If she fails to have this capacity in *C1*, then she is not morally responsible for her action in that context. According to Vargas, this question is answered by considering other *possible* contexts that are "relevantly similar" to the Applebee's context. If, in a "suitable proportion" of these relevantly similar contexts, Alex can exercise control over her actions, then she would seem to have the capacity for volitional control in *C1*.[13] Let's pursue the matter just a bit further.

Later that week Alex finds herself in a different setting *C2* at the grocery store to do her weekly shopping. At this time it would seem that Alex is in a context "relevantly similar" to *C1* the restaurant. At the grocery store Alex continues to recognize and endorse all of the relevant moral considerations cited previously in *C1* about the value of health, the importance of eating nutritional food, and the high sugar content of soda, in particular, the belief that she ought not to drink soda if she wants to lose weight and become healthier. She remembers her resolution to purchase healthier food and avoids the soda aisle altogether. At this time she does not buy a six-pack of Coke because she believes that in order to live a healthier lifestyle—a value she endorses—she ought not to drink sugary beverages. So, even though Alex does not exercise her capacity for volitional control with respect to her action in *C1* at the restaurant, we see that she is capable of doing so in a context that is relevantly similar to the restaurant setting; a context where she is also faced with the decision about whether or not to buy and consume sugary drinks. And in order to accommodate Vargas's further condition, let us also suppose that there are a "suitable proportion" of relevantly similar contexts where Alex does detect the moral considerations cited above, and is motivated to act for those reasons, and successfully acts accordingly. Hence, because Alex is capable of volitional control in a suitable proportion of contexts that are relevantly similar to *C1*, she does satisfy the volitional control condition. Thus, she is morally responsible for her action of purchasing the soda in the context *C1* at Applebee's.[14] So far, so good. But for many other obese individuals, the circumstances that affect choices about what to eat, and how much, are more complicated.

Case study: *Fat Boy, Thin Man*

In his memoir *Fat Boy, Thin Man*, Michael Prager (2010) honestly and poignantly characterizes his lifetime struggle with obesity. This personal account exhibits some features of a food justice narrative we have identified in earlier chapters. Specifically, in Prager's commentary about his own life we have the resources to challenge the moral fault narrative that individual people alone are morally and personally responsible for their condition of obesity. This is possible because the reader's point of view is from the inside as Prager details what it is like to live with constant cravings for food and to fail to curtail his eating over and over again. The *particularity* achieved is created by Prager's first-person testimony, and this positions us to more accurately *construe* a judgment about moral responsibility in circumstances that are specific to person and place. In other words, from the reader's inside point of view we can make judgments about the moral responsibility of a situated agent.

Even though Prager characterizes himself as a "food addict," he is determined to convince the reader that he assumes personal responsibility for his condition.

> **The reliable way out of obesity is via personal responsibility.** This point has been lost on the hundreds of folks who have railed against my arguments for food addiction in periodicals, so I'm eager to make it here: No one but me put the food in my mouth. Even if I had grown up imprisoned in a crawl space under the basement stairs (I wasn't), even if tragedy has befallen me every 15 minutes since (it hasn't), I'm still responsible for what I eat. If my food is out of control (it was), then I'm responsible for finding, requesting, and accepting the help I need. (Prager 2010, 26)

Nonetheless, when Prager describes himself as a "food addict" he is presenting a competing narrative about the limits of personal responsibility and the inadequacy of characterizing obesity in all cases as a moral failing. One way of understanding the kind of agency implied by food addiction is to see things from the point of view of the agent himself, paying particular attention to how issues of choice and control are described.[15] For example, Prager (2010, 22–3) writes:

> **Problem eater or addict; what's the difference?** In a word, choice. I began abusing substances other than food in junior high, beginning with cigarettes and eventually getting to marijuana and cocaine. I dabbled in alcohol, amphetamines, barbiturates, and acid, as well … I don't take any of those substances any more. I stopped cigarettes when Ronald Reagan doubled the federal cigarette tax. I stopped cocaine, when I finally realized that I would never, ever, get enough of it, no matter how much time, money, or attention I devoted to it. I stopped pot on no more impetus than a writing assignment I was given while in rehab.
>
> In each case, I decided to stop—and then actually did! Addicts often "decide" to stop, but rarely try, or succeed if they do. Meanwhile, I've sworn off food on many "morning afters," only to be back in the food by mid-morning. I have never been [able] to "just eat less," not in the long term, not as a natural act. Unchecked, my eating will always expand, and so will my body, grotesquely. This is undeniable.
>
> Some people are born with a predisposition to addiction, but anyone can develop it. It's not necessarily a linear process, and it's not inevitable once it's begun. *But there is the point after which all choice is lost.* (My italics)

In his article, "Addiction, Paradox, and the Good I Would," Richard Garrett (2011) also characterizes his own experiences with food as "addictive." Garrett describes this kind of addiction as a pattern of behavior that is voluntary but not "sufficiently controlled by the really *good* and *important* consequences that would follow from abstention." Instead momentary pleasures prevail even when the addict's reason tells him that the long-term consequences of his behavior are extremely harmful. In short, the food addict's behavior is not "rationally voluntary."[16] Garrett remarks, "Reason becomes impotent at such moments" (p. 253). One conclusion we may draw from these depictions of the lived experience of the food addict is that the agent's choices are significantly compromised by internal desires that override his rational assessment about what to eat and how much to eat. What remains to be seen is how this kind of diminished control over thinking and acting about food choices affects our moral appraisals about the agent's responsibility.[17]

Prager describes many moments in his tortured relationship with food that can be characterized as failed exercises of volitional control. Here is one such description:

> When I was assigned to the night shift to help produce a morning edition of the paper that would be edited in Painesville but assembled 20 miles away, it institutionalized two eating session into every working day.
>
> I'd graze at a low level on the way to the paste-up shop, perhaps getting a couple extra bags of chips when I stopped for the takeout dinner I'd eat at my desk. It was as close to controlled eating as I got; I found that if I dived in too deeply, I would not only be uncomfortable in my desk chair, but I would be unable to concentrate on the work to be done. So I indulged in the food equivalent of the three-martini lunch, enough to take the edge off without going over it.
>
> But the buy for the ride back home was different. We'd be done by 11 or so, and I'd indulge in the relief of knowing that I owed the world no more that day and could now eat with abandon.
>
> Before the ride home, which I'd share with Larry King when he was the Mutual Radio Network's overnight man, I'd stop at one of the mini-marts on Route 20 in search of two types of food: For the road, I wanted nothing that needed heating or assembling, and enough of it to last the 30-minute journey. But I also needed enough to get me through to morning without having to go out again. (Prager 2010, 48–9)

Let's specify context *C1* to be the circumstance where Prager purchases chips and other ready to eat food at a mini-mart on his way home from work. We might also build into the example that Prager has no difficulty *detecting* the moral considerations that favor eating healthy food in the right proportions. But *C1* is a case where he fails to exercise control over his eating. Does Prager have the *capacity* for volitional control? Recall that in the basic illustrative example involving Alex we answered that question by imagining other possible contexts. Because we judged that Alex could exercise control in a "suitable proportion" of contexts that are relevantly similar to buying and consuming the Coke at Applebee's, this implied that Alex did have the *capacity* for volitional control, even though she failed to exercise this capacity in the Applebee's context. But Prager's case is different. On most occasions when he is in a situation to purchase and eat large amounts of processed food, he does so. According to Prager, there are a suitable proportion of relevantly similar contexts to *C1* where he fails to exercise volitional control in buying and consuming large amounts of junk food, despite knowing that this is not what he ought to do in order to become healthy. This is evidence that Prager fails to have the capacity for volitional control over what he eats and how much in context *C1* and in other possible contexts that are relevantly similar to this set of circumstances. If so, then Prager is not morally responsible for his actions in *C1* that causally contribute to his condition of obesity. Recall that this is so because on Vargas's account of moral responsibility, an agent is morally responsible for an action only if he has the capacity for detecting moral considerations that favor healthy eating, and he also has the capacity for volitional control over what he eats and how much.

One puzzling feature of the conclusion that Prager fails to have the capacity for volitional control about what and how much he eats is that it makes mysterious Prager's recovery from food addiction. In other words, it is part of Prager's story that he eventually manages his food choices, loses weight, and recovers control over these aspects of his life. But does not this show that he *does* have the capacity for volitional control over what and how much he eats? The answer to this question depends on how we understand what it means for an agent to satisfy the volitional control condition in "a suitable proportion of relevantly similar contexts" to the actual circumstance of *C1*, where Prager purchases junk food at the mini-mart on the way home from work. So one challenge is to say what counts as a relevantly similar context to *C1*.

To answer this question suppose we judged similarity of context by imaging the number and kinds of facts about the world that must change in order for Prager to recover from patterns of unhealthy eating.[18] Prager (2010, 48) alerts us to how the food environment created ideal conditions for his overeating.

More often than grocery stores and drive-throughs, though, I frequented convenience stores, which reached just the right spot in my addict brain:

- They are ubiquitous, which means a fix is never far away.
- Unless someone is in line in front of you, the gratification is instant.
- They are stocked disproportionately with junk food.
- They have high staff turnover, which means you are less likely to experience the disdain in the eyes of your dealer.

Obviously, Prager's recovery could not depend on avoiding all food like the alcoholic might avoid alcohol altogether. But what his particular form of treatment required was avoiding certain "trigger" foods that led him to fits of binging; namely, those foods containing refined sugar and refined starches (Prager 2010, 128). Prager admits that these foods were his downfall, over and over again. Junk food was easy enough to find in the numerous convenience stores he frequented near his home or when traveling. But simply trying to avoid junk food was not enough. In addition, Prager's (and Garrett's) recovery was made possible by the choice to enter into professional therapy and counseling (over many years), or a spiritual twelve-step program, in combination with the involvement of loving friends and family. Call these circumstances necessary for Prager's recovery *C2*. It seems clear that a significant number of features of the world need to change in order for Prager to achieve recovery from unhealthy food choices. This recovery did not merely involve saving himself by making better choices about food on particular occasions, or by merely "trying harder," or by taking more personal responsibility for his diet. Prager's recovery from addictive patterns of behavior involving unhealthy eating was made possible only with a considerable amount of social support, therapeutic intervention, and by altogether avoiding the ubiquitous toxic food environment.[19] The cautious conclusion here is that the circumstances in *C2* are not relevantly similar to context *C1*. Why again does this matter? This conclusion allows us to say two plausible things about Prager's plight. First, he fails to have the capacity for volitional control over what to eat, and how much, in context *C1*. This means he is not morally responsible for his actions in that context. Second, this account of situated agency does not compromise Prager's capacity for volitional control, in general. We can still say with confidence that in some contexts Prager can exercise volitional control over his unhealthy patterns of eating. As we have seen, what makes recovery possible for Prager (and others similarly situated) are significant changes in the external food environment, social support systems, and therapeutic interventions.

What is significant about this case study is that it makes visible the limitations of the moral fault narrative when applied to obesity discourse. It does so by shifting the locus of moral responsibility for being obese from the individual, to those external circumstances that shape an agent's control over his food choices. Judging that a moral agent has the capacity for volitional control just depends on these external circumstances. A food justice narrative more completely profiles these background conditions as part of what it means to be morally responsible for those actions that contribute to the condition of being obese. Of course, not all cases of obesity can be explained by the special circumstances of food addiction.

Case study: *Fed Up*

In the documentary film, *Fed Up* (Soechtig 2014), we meet a number of children who tell us in their own words what it is like to struggle with obesity. I use this film as an illustrative case study—one that qualifies as a food justice narrative for the following reasons. First, it challenges a popular master narrative about obesity that characterizes this condition as a moral failing involving a person's lack of willpower, character faults like laziness or sloth, or some other lapse of personal responsibility for one's health. Second, the film offers us an alternative picture or story about the causes of obesity that display three features of a food justice narrative—particularity, emotional engagement, and accuracy. First, particularity is achieved by inviting us into the lives of individual children who are willing to describe their lived experience of being obese. These stories are poignant reminders that the "obesity epidemic" is not merely describable by citing general statistics, demographics, and financial costs of medical care and associated diseases. The inside look at the problem of obesity is contextualized by interviews with family members, seeing up close what is on offer in the school cafeteria, observing food purchases and food preparation in the culture of each home, and even witnessing the particular exercise routines attempted by the children interviewed. Second, in displaying these details the film also skillfully creates an emotional response in the viewer that encourages our sympathies toward each child who tells his or her story. Third, by focusing on the emotional aspects of individual obese children and the particular obstacles they face in trying to lose weight, the film guides us to a more discerning construal or evaluation of the moral responsibility of those who are struggling with obesity in the context of real-world circumstances that affect their food choices.

Meet Brady Kluge from Easly, South Carolina. He is fifteen years old and weighs 215 pounds. Brady knows that he needs to lose weight but admits that "I'm failing." He cannot understand how his younger brother can eat exactly the same foods but does not appear unhealthy or overweight. Maggie Valentine is twelve years old and weighs 212 pounds. She confides to the camera that she is an example of a person devoted to exercising and eating healthy food. We see her swimming, riding a bike, and walking the dog. But she admits that she cannot lose weight. This constant trying and not succeeding is what is frustrating and entirely inexplicable to her. Joe Lopez is fourteen years old, and lives in Houston, Texas. His failed attempts to lose weight over many years make him eligible for weight reduction surgery. According to his physician, at the rate he is gaining he is likely to be dead at twenty years from obesity related diseases. What makes these stories especially poignant is that each child sees his or her condition of obesity as a personal failure. Each has heard the mantra that the solution to his or her plight is to "eat less, exercise more." Each has accepted the truth of the saying, "You are what you eat" and "It's up to you to try harder." It is heartbreaking to witness just how psychologically damaging the *moral fault narrative* is when internalized by these children. The narrator remarks, "They are torturing themselves to do the cure. But it is the wrong cure. It's a crime." The "wrong cure" in this case is the theory of energy balance, or the simple formula of calories in and calories out. According to the narrators, what is false about this explanation is that not all calories are equal. Many believe now that different carbohydrates such as glucose and fructose metabolize differently in the body leading to different physiological responses, especially differences in the accumulation of fat. This view implies, for example, that the body accumulates more fat from the consumption of 150 calories of a sugary beverage compared to the consumption of 150 calories of kale or almonds (Taubes 2017; Nestle and Nesheim 2012). If true, the recommendations to "work off" the calories consumed will never realistically solve the problem of obesity.

What this food justice narrative creates for the viewer is a sympathetic lens through which we can evaluate the moral fault narrative. We may still believe that there are choices that each child ought to make that are consistent with healthy eating. But it is very difficult to hold Brady, Maggie, and Joe morally responsible for their condition of obesity once we see the combination of conditions that contribute to their continuing slide into ill health. This emotional connection is encouraged by the narrators who tell us that, "The deck is stacked against them." The wider set of circumstances that permit us to challenge the universal truth of the moral fault narrative contextualizes exactly how individual food choices are influenced. Importantly, for our moral evaluation, Brady and others have no control over these situational conditions.

Consider the well-documented fact that there is limited access to nutritious food which prohibits those who are, in principle, free to choose something other than processed food but are, in practice, unable to travel to sites where nutritious food is sold. This is because nutritious food is not available in many low-income neighborhoods, or there is limited transportation to retail grocery stores or to farmer's markets. Even if the problem of access to nutritious food is solved there is still the basic fact that many people may not have the money or time to locate it and cook it. James Behnke, former Pillsbury executive says, "We're hooked on inexpensive food, just like we're hooked on cheap energy. The real question is this price sensitivity and, unfortunately, the growing disparity of income between the haves and have-nots. It costs more money to eat fresher, healthier foods. And so, there is a huge economic issue involved in the obesity problem" (Moss 2013). In principle we may only need knowledge about what is better for us to eat in order to improve our diets. But this idea is based on the mistaken assumption that we are each equally free in the relevant sense to choose nutritious food.[20]

For example, between the years 1974–2000 we have doubled our intake of sugar. This is not surprising since 80 percent of the food now sold in grocery store aisles have increased amounts of sugar. The school lunch cafeterias in public schools where these children eat offer fries, pizza, chips, and soda. In many cases the schools have negotiated deals with fast food outlets to supply children with school lunches. The narrators of *Fed Up* tell us that the food and beverage industry has infiltrated public schools with foods that are making our children sick. We now know that in 2002 the World Health Organization (WHO), responsible for setting global health standards, produced a technical document stating that sugar is the main cause of obesity. The sugar industry pushed back hard to stop the report, and the WHO guidelines warning about the consumption of sugar were deleted from the document by successful lobbying (O'Connor 2016). As the narrator of the film adds, by resisting the regulation of sugar, and by advertising and marketing sugary foods directly to children, the food industry is exploiting the vulnerability of children. "We've put private profit and special interest ahead of health."[21]

Given these background conditions, the difficult question is how to assess the moral responsibility of the children who seem unable to lose weight. Some criteria are needed beyond our sympathetic responses to the plights of the children profiled in the film. The account of moral responsibility offered by Vargas is helpful here as well. Let's focus specifically on the volitional control part of this account of responsibility using Brady Kluge as the agent. When Brady eats chips and a soda for a snack after school, does he just demonstrate lack of willpower in this context *C1*, or does he fail to have the capacity for volitional control in this context? If Brady does have the capacity for volitional control in *C1*, then he is morally responsible for eating unhealthy food in this context, provided that he knows and understands the moral considerations that favor healthy eating. But in order to evaluate whether or not Brady has the capacity for volitional control in *C1*, we need to look at a suitable number of possible contexts that are relevantly similar to this one. Based on how he reports his difficulties in the film it is reasonable to say that in many other settings that are similar to *C1*, Brady also eats unhealthy food. When the school lunch offers pizza and fries, he eats these also. When he goes out with his friends or family for an affordable meal, he eats a hamburger, fries, and a Coke. When his parents buy packaged foods in the grocery stores, these items are invariably loaded with sugar, and this is what he eats at home. As Brady himself says, "When you are close to it, you just want it." The conclusion I draw from these first-person reports is that Brady (and others who are similarly situated) lack the capacity for volitional control over healthy eating since there are few healthy food choices that Brady can make in these various contexts where he attempts to choose what to eat and how much. And if the conditions that create unhealthy food choices are out of Brady's control, then this means that in context *C1* Brady is not morally responsible for his failure to eat a healthy snack.

It is important to be precise about just what this moral appraisal means with respect to individual agency. It does not imply that Brady has no choices whatsoever to eat healthy food. Nor does it imply that his general capacities of control are diminished overall. What does make sense to say is that Brady (and many others similarly situated) choose what and how much to eat in many situations where these choices are few, and include mostly processed foods high in sugar and salt. Vargas's theory of responsibility allows us to focus on just those circumstances that create and shape this kind of diminished capacity for control. But instead of pointing to the very strong internal desires of the food addict as we did in the case of Prager and Garrett, we are here profiling the external constraints on choice that characterize the situations of Brady and others; namely, the "built" food environment.[22]

Extending the scope of responsibility

One advantage of employing the analysis of responsibility recommended here is that we may be more cautious about using the moral fault narrative to describe all people who are obese without regard to the circumstances that affect that person's capacity to freely choose what and how much to eat. But the further advantage gained is to bring into clearer focus those background conditions that compromise moral agency. By seeing what contributes to diminished moral agency we can more easily extend the scope of responsibility beyond the personal responsibility of individuals to institutions, policies, and corporate players (Nestle 2015). Vargas (2013b, 343) remarks:

> In particular, it is important to recognize that societies, states, and cultures all structure our actual capacities. Being raised in an antiracist context plays a role in enhancing sensitivity to moral considerations tied to antiracist concerns. Similarly, being raised in a sexist, fascist, or classist culture will ordinarily shape a person's incapacities to respond to egalitarian concerns. Such considerations may suggest that we need to ask whether societies or states have some kind of moral, practical, or political obligation to endeavor to shape the circumstances of actors in ways that insulate them against situational effects that degrade their (moral or other) reasoning. We might go on to ask whether societies or states have commensurate obligations to foster contexts that enhance our rational and moral agency. If they do, it suggests that free will is less a matter of science than it is of politics or morality.

Here Vargas asks a general rhetorical question about whether or not states and societies may be morally implicated in structuring our capacities to detect moral considerations and for self-governance. But the question has critical bite in the context of this real-world issue about obesity. Institutions and states design and implement public health policies, allow for corporate manipulation of consumers by the food industry, tolerate fundamental inequalities that sustain conditions of poverty and diminish access to health care, education, affordable housing, and increase exposure to toxic food and polluted environments. To the extent that these policies, corporate actors, and representatives of government create obstacles to moral agency, they are morally blameworthy.[23] Of course, this claim reaches beyond obesity discourse and obesity prevention policies. The point of demanding that such conditions be honored is to optimize the circumstances necessary for all moral agents to exercise their agency, not just those who are overweight.

Vargas uses the expression "moral architecture" to refer to the possibility of intentionally shaping and cultivating those conditions that structure our actual capacities that are conducive to responsible agency.[24] How might moral architecture be implemented in our particular study of obesity and responsibility? One epistemic obstacle is the general population's inability to *see* and understand how situational conditions circumscribe agency and, in some cases, exempt individuals from moral responsibility. As we have seen, food justice narratives can perform this illustrative function by including the particular circumstances of a person's life that illustrate how an individual is situated in, and influenced by, structural background conditions that constrain choices and limit opportunities to act. This kind of story reminds us that particular populations of people retain their agency even as their choices are limited by the combined effect of these structural background conditions.[25] In this context the real explanatory value of such stories will be to reveal the extent to which our food choices are shaped by conditions that are largely out of the control of individual eaters.

Conclusion

Let's return to the two main reasons for seeking greater conceptual clarity about how "personal responsibility" is used in obesity discourse. One rationale for doing so is that in these settings the concept of moral responsibility rarely comes equipped with any criteria of application. Now that we have introduced a *revisionist reasons* account of responsibility we see how the control condition especially can be used to decide how moral responsibility applies to obese individuals. Brady Kluge, Maggie Valentine, and Joe Lopez occupy a social and political location that contributes to undermining their respective capacities for volitional control in a wide range of contexts where each may recognize reasons for choosing to eat healthy food but cannot act accordingly. While not every individual who is obese can be exempted from moral responsibility for their food choices, these children surely represent a large population of actual people who find themselves in a similar set of circumstances. What is significant about this conclusion is that contrary to what some believe, the property of being obese does not single out a class of individuals who are also morally responsible for their condition of obesity. Instead the way we determine attributions of responsibility is explained by having the capacity to detect moral considerations relevant to action, and having the capacity for volitional control over the actions that these moral considerations favor. Attributions of responsibility are made about an agent's capacities in actual and possible circumstances that are relevantly similar. So if moral exemptions apply in the way I have argued, then a large number of individuals who are obese do not deserve to be the targets of moral blame, nor do they deserve the moral indignation that is sometimes directed towards them.

This account of situated agency also meets the second demand for the project undertaken here which is to resist the following false dichotomy; either individuals are fully morally responsible for being obese, or they are altogether exempt from responsibility. Describing the circumstances of situated agents in judging attributions of responsibility allows us to include in our moral appraisal structural background conditions that limit knowledge and constrain freedoms and opportunities. But in doing so there is no need to choose between either holding a person morally responsible or blaming the food environment instead. The situated agency of individuals allows us to make this contextual analysis without forcing a choice between these two extreme positions about responsibility. In other words, the particular theory of responsibility applied here offers us a more nuanced and realistic way of understanding how to assign moral responsibility to an agent who is situated in contexts that variously effect that agent's ability to detect moral considerations, and to successfully act in accordance with these moral considerations.

I conclude this chapter with the following disclaimer. Michael Prager, Brady, Maggie, and Joe only incompletely represent the class of all obese people who decide what to eat, and attempt to act on their food choices. By using these few case studies I do not pretend to capture all of the real-world circumstances relevant to the moral appraisal of this population. Even so the analysis here suggests that we have sufficient theoretical resources to resist the presumption that all obese individuals are appropriate targets for moral disapprobation.

Mother Hubbard's Cupboard: Erin

Erin is the MHC food pantry and volunteer coordinator. For a few weeks now I have been taking her instructions about what to shop for at the Food Bank, and she is the main organizer of food in the pantry, as well as helping the novice volunteers, like me, get started. On a Thursday, after Patrick and I unloaded a relatively light load from the Food Bank into the pantry, she graciously agreed to talk with me about her story.

How did you get started working at the MHC?

Erin arrived in Bloomington about five years ago when she was working for another nonprofit organization that created and sustained transitional housing for youth. At that time she had a one-year contract with AmeriCorps Vista. As part of this program she had agreed to live in poverty. Members of AmeriCorps are asked to *live on about US$ 750 a month to pay all of their expenses including, rent, utilities, food, car insurance, etc. Erin said it was close to impossible to manage this. She was on food stamps during that time, and her first visit to Mother Hubbard was as a client. She came to shop. And she remembers saying to herself, "This is what it feels like to ask for food."*

When a management position opened up at the MHC, she applied. She immediately saw how unique the organization was. It does provide emergency services and tries to meet the basic needs of members of the community, but what Erin likes most about MHC is that it is not just an emergency service. There is also the nutritional education program, gardening programs, food preparation classes, and so on. "We are teaching a person to fish, but we also give fish. And giving fish is like saying; here is one less stress in your life that you have to deal with."

What do you like now about what you do? What are the challenges you face, or the worst parts of your job?

Even though Erin begins by saying that she likes her job a lot, she brings her remarks quickly around to what she regards as problematic.

"The danger is that these (nonprofit) organizations are just a band aid. It breaks my heart that families I met four years ago are still coming in. What can we do for these people other than to just supply a constant food source? This is the part that doesn't feel good."

"For example, we received a beautiful hand written note from a woman who said, 'Thank you for keeping me alive.' But what would happen if we disappeared? This is the most frustrating aspect of my job."

"What I've noticed in the last four years of working at MHC is generational poverty. Parents with children under ten years old have been shopping here since I arrived. And what that means is that for these children, this is a normal way of life. Getting food stamps, filling out forms for social work agencies to get housing, going to the food pantry; all of this is creating a normalcy around what it means to grow up poor. And there should be something else. There should be educational opportunities for kids in order to create something other than this kind of life; something to encourage them to break out of this cycle."

Then Erin says with all seriousness, "What we need is a complete overhaul of society and government. We need to become less reliant on these larger food systems and consumerism." Finally coming back to what she does love about her job, Erin adds, "40% of our clients garden at home, so we are having some influence on different ways of eating. MHC has classes on gardening, preserving food, how to prepare food from the garden. And this is a contribution to some alternative way of living; one that is less expensive in terms of transportation costs, energy, and one that is just more environmentally friendly."

So, where do you go from here? What do you imagine yourself doing in the future?

"Well, I have my B.A. in English and I've been working in nonprofits for six years now. The space we have now at the MHC is too small for what I imagine. We are hearing today about a lease on a larger building (shh . . . no one knows this yet), and if we get this space then I want to focus more on kids and literacy. Maybe we can have more books, reading time, and just more attention paid to education. Because if kids know how to read, if they learn to love to read, then they will do better in school. And this will make all the difference in what they imagine is possible for themselves."

Erin pauses to think about this for a minute.

"I really want to do something that changes the structure of society. There is such an imbalance, such a huge disparity between those that do have power and money and influence, and those who don't. The same is true in government. Those people who have money and power are the same ones who are making policy decisions. That has to change for us to be successful."

I ask Erin if maybe she herself is interested in politics.

"I did run for local office for the county council a while ago. I think the potential is there to make some changes in local government settings because local politics can actually be functional and you can also impact a large number of people in the community. The scale is manageable since you can identify a need, and actually see how or if it is being met. But government on a larger scale? No. I'm not interested in that. It's too big and really I don't believe in participating in that system."

"I want to work on the revolutionary side," she says with a grin.

"What I want to do in the future is to travel. I want to see how other countries and governments are handling these problems about need and service. Then I want to come up with a grand scheme about how to save the world."

We both chuckle in a wry sort of way, rolling our eyes just a bit to acknowledge how idealistic this sounds. But my own opinion of Erin is that she will do something that counts as "saving the world." I don't actually say this to her but I feel so moved that I almost reach out and hug her.

So, what advice would you give to young people (or older ones)?

"Pay attention to what is going on in the world. It's difficult to tell sometimes. But be certain you can trust where you get your information. How reliable is the news source? Pay attention to things that actually matter, like suffering. We make choices all the time that contribute to people's suffering, like the clothes we buy, the cars we drive, the food we eat. Just be mindful of the effects of your choices and actions."

7

Practicing Philosophy

The individual stories included here focus on the particular lived experiences of individuals who are hungry, who work in the fields to pick our food, and those who suffer from obesity. These stories create vivid snapshots of injustice. But the *moral purpose* of seeing injustice revealed in these ways is to position the activist to take responsibility for justice. Let's review where we are, and how we got here.

As I have illustrated throughout, some realistic narratives about food (documentary films, memoirs, and ethnographies) can educate us ethically by developing in the reader or viewer a skill to more accurately see existing injustices in the food system such as structural injustice and oppression. The skill model of ethical expertise explained in Chapter 2 recommends to the ethical novice to develop a moral discernment to "read the situation." The vehicle for developing ethical expertise is the particular concrete case which comes equipped with context and complicating circumstances. It is in this setting that the meanings of ethical concepts like fair and unfair, just and unjust, get their meanings by application to practical living. So the skills needed for the ethical novice, as well as for the ethical expert, are comparative judgments about the story particulars. One kind of story might capture a paradigmatic case of injustice such as exploitation. If so, we should ask what features this case shares with other particular examples. In this way by comparing the ethical particulars displayed by the story and, by judging relative similarities between them, the ethical novice learns how to extend the relevant moral concept of injustice to new cases.

The role of stories

I have argued throughout that learning to see what matters ethically about the particular case is facilitated by attending to the essential features of a special class of realistic stories that I call *food justice narratives*. Food justice narratives answer to the demand of educating us ethically by satisfying three conditions; namely, particularity, emotional engagement, and accuracy. For example, a food justice narrative should include those particular details about the identity of those who attempt to nourish themselves, as well as obstacles that prevent individuals from doing so. And it should include in the story itself the background circumstances about constraints on free agency that make it difficult to live well. A food justice narrative should also invite the reader or viewer to look at things from the inside by depicting the emotional texture of a human life and, by doing so, encourage us to engage and educate our emotions of sympathy and compassion. And ideally a food justice narrative should satisfy accuracy conditions. First, this kind of realistic narrative should be factually correct, supported by evidence that neither distorts nor misrepresents the lives of people who are depicted in the narrative. Second, a judgment about accuracy means that we can make a plausibly correct moral appraisal, allowing us to apply concepts about fairness, justice, or what is morally right with some confidence. There is still the possibility that the condition of accuracy (both factual and moral construal) will not be realized perfectly in a food justice narrative. Writing or reading a food justice narrative, by itself, does not guarantee moral truth. But this kind of promise is unrealistic for any ethical theory or methodology. What we can reasonably expect is that a food justice narrative will locate an attentive reader epistemically to understand what master narratives obfuscate or misrepresent.

In addition to satisfying these three conditions described above (particularity, emotional engagement, and accuracy), there is a corrective role that food justice narratives play. Consider the two main kinds of stories profiled here. One kind of story I have classified as a *master narrative* about food. In general, master narratives are "socially shared" understandings of the world that depict individuals or sub groups in ways that are familiar—conforming to "stock plots and character types"—as well as stereotypical representations, since they often include some unexamined assumptions about our common cultural experiences. The main reason for taking precautions about master narratives is that they sometimes give expression to oppressive ideologies that target individuals and the sub groups to which they belong. In this way master narratives can contribute to loss of respect, truncated moral agency, and limitations on opportunities to live well for these populations. It is useful in this conclusion to briefly review the master narratives about food discussed throughout earlier chapters. In this way we can look across examples to see what they may have in common and consider the way in which they contribute to ethical damage.

Chapter 3 profiles master narratives about food insecurity that characterize hunger as the outcome when someone has suffered some tragic accidental misfortune interfering with her ability to provide food for herself and her family. Another feature of this kind of popular story characterizes those who are food-insecure as morally innocent who, by their fortitude, hard work, and virtuous characters, manage to recover from a temporary loss of control over the contingent circumstances of their lives. Each version of this story illustrates a damaging master narrative insofar as it interferes with an ordinary citizen's understanding of the need for advocacy and justice, although in slightly different ways. In the latter case, if we characterize those who are food-insecure as ideal moral agents who represent the paradigm of need, then we may be tempted to exclude those who fail to meet this innocence standard. For example, we may come to believe that the majority of those who are poor and hungry are essentially different than us and in some way morally at fault. This idea contributes to the belief that inequality is a natural outcome of poor choices or a failure of moral character. We may pity those who are hungry and continue to feed them through acts of charity, but we may not believe that changes in public policy and advocating for political justice are necessary because in these cases it is not deserved.

Alternatively, individual stories that imply food insecurity is a temporary and accidental misfortune implies that under normal circumstances most of us can realize our responsibilities to work and feed ourselves. These stories suggest that ordinary circumstances sometimes go awry, creating obstacles to living well through no fault of those individuals who suffer the consequences. In fact, we may well imagine that life could have gone the same way for any one of us—a series of unfortunate events due to illness and accidents that create obstacles to living well. In this account of things we may believe that those who suffer food insecurity are morally deserving. But this kind of master narrative preserves our inclinations to extend food charity in one form or another rather than motivating us to undertake responsibility for justice. Indeed, this is a reasonable response since accidental tragedy and misfortune are not states of affairs that we can guard against by changes in public policy. While well intentioned, these stories about accidental misfortune obscure fundamental explanations about the causes and conditions of hunger that apply systematically to groups of people. The salient feature of both versions of this master narrative is that they appear to explain the complex social, economic, and political conditions of food insecurity by reference to individual people and the idiosyncratic actions and events that surround their particular lives. This kind of explanation obscures the need for political justice.

In Chapter 5, ethnographer Seth Holmes (2013) profiles damaging master narratives about migrant farmworkers. I examined the following three kinds of stories, in particular. First, because it is assumed that labor migration is owed to economic pressures, it is also believed that indigenous Mexicans migrate to the United States voluntarily. By assuming that migrant workers can do otherwise than to advance their economic status, it is sometimes implied that whatever risks or fate they suffer here are freely assumed. The second ethically damaging narrative about migrant farmworkers makes invisible their humanity. When they are treated unfairly or in ways that are oppressive and exploitative, this unjust treatment is described as natural or deserved. In this way a moral justification operates to entrench a social, economic, and political hierarchy with migrant workers occupying the lowest rung of this hierarchy. This constitutes a deprivation of opportunity for farmworkers to improve their income, job, or status. A third kind of story that counts as ethically injurious is the assumption that moral agency operates entirely freely and unencumbered. One consequence of this supposition is that farmworkers are believed to be individually responsible for their position in the hierarchy of labor. One illustration described by Holmes is healthcare. In some cases the ill health of farmworkers is explained by their presumed free choices to work in the fields where their bodies are subjected to physical deterioration. Some health professionals fail to recognize the social determinants of health problems suffered by migrant farmworkers and, especially, how social and economic forces shape and sustain ill health. In this way individual agency is stripped of context about work, health, housing, and education, making it more likely that individual people are blamed for their plights, rather than structural conditions that unfairly disadvantage populations of people.

In Chapter 6, the source of ethical damage is a "moral fault narrative" about obesity and personal responsibility. In some cases personal responsibility discourse assumes the form of moral approbation and blame assigned to the population of obese individuals. This kind of story charges obese people with moral failure for not living a healthy lifestyle, or by not exhibiting a sufficient degree of control over what and how much to eat. The ethical injury here is that all obese people are targeted for moral blame because of the shape of their bodies.

One common theme emerges from close scrutiny of these various master narratives. In all of these cases we discern a distorted or misrepresentative explanation created about who is hungry and why, how migrant farmworkers should be treated, and the moral appraisal of those who are obese. This misrepresentation is created by a disproportionate emphasis on the personal responsibility of individual people; the idiosyncratic misfortunes that create food insecurity, a migrant worker's failure to protect himself from suffering, poverty, and ill health, or an obese person's inability to take responsibility for her condition of obesity. These stories create ethical damage by assuming that individual people exist in social, political, and economic isolation. When structural background circumstances are invisible to the consumer of these stories, then she will fail to see and understand how these contextual circumstances constrain choices or create obstacles that interfere or impede successful action. The cost of ignoring these background conditions is that food justice in each of these domains is compromised. We will not formulate political, institutional, and sustainable policy solutions to hunger by focusing only on an individual person's accidental tragedies of living. We will not institutionalize just immigration policies and the fair treatment of those who pick our food if we fail to see migrant workers as dignified human beings deserving of our respect. And we will not understand how corporate players and powerful special interests influence our diets by focusing solely on the personal responsibility of obese individuals.

Once we clearly see the ethical damage created by master narratives about food we are well positioned to appreciate another kind of story that I have described and illustrated throughout. Recall that we are using the concept of a counterstory (Nelson 2001) to capture the *narrative act* of a food justice narrative, or what it is done with the story. And what is done with a food justice narrative is to resist or to rewrite a particular master narrative in such a way as to correct the ethical damage or oppressive ideology created. The case studies I have profiled in Chapters 4–6 function exactly in this way. What kind of narrative correction do they demonstrate?

In Chapter 4, a food justice narrative challenges a master narrative about who is hungry and why. The case study used to illustrate this is the documentary film, *A Place at the Table* (Jacobson and Silverbush 2013). Barbie is one character in this film whose hunger is shaped by structural conditions over which she has no control. These background conditions include USDA subsidies to commodity crops, lobbying by agribusiness, decreased funding for SNAP benefits, National School Lunch, housing subsidies, programs for seniors, and Aid to Families with Dependent Children—that support those living at the margins of society (Jacobson and Silverbush 2013). By profiling these background conditions as part of a deeper explanation of food insecurity we effectively rewrite the hunger narrative. Instead of emphasizing the contingencies of living that create accidental and personal misfortune, the new understanding achieved by this food justice narrative is how food insecurity is created by a complex array of structural conditions that are shaped by economic and political policies. This larger explanatory framework linking poverty and food insecurity is not depicted as inevitable or invulnerable to change. Instead the film intentionally presents us with a more accurate epistemic vantage point for the ethical scrutiny and review of public policy, laws, corporate power and influence, and political ideology. This positions the viewer for food justice political activism.

Likewise, a food justice narrative on the website of The Hunger Project corrects some potentially misrepresentative stories about global food insecurity. In the success stories profiled here the attentive reader comes to understand how sustainable solutions to hunger are intimately connected to other conditions that make this possible. In particular, the story of Sankura Slamata from Burkina Faso illustrates her initiative to create a market garden to sell vegetables to the community. This does suggest individual initiative and hard work. But the more complete explanation of her success is owed to the fact that she received skills training, and that a local microcredit financial organization helped finance the purchase of seeds for her garden market. The background conditions for successful and sustainable solutions to global hunger include empowering girls to have opportunities to be educated and healthy, initiatives to address environmental problems, and include programs that focus on gender discrimination in those settings where women and girls are unequally impeded in their opportunities to work or to be educated. Local initiatives also promote partnering with political institutions, improving nutrition and access to clean water and better sanitation, and addressing poverty and food prices. These are just some of the structural conditions that The Hunger Project identifies as central to creating sustainable solutions to global hunger. Including these background conditions as part of the story about how to address food insecurity shifts the reader's focus from individual personal responsibility and hard work, to other necessary conditions that must be satisfied to ensure the global right to food.

In Chapter 5, a food justice narrative illustrates how to correct misrepresentative and sometimes false stories about labor migration, and stories that make invisible the humanity of migrant farmworkers. In his moving ethnography, *Fresh Fruit, Broken Bodies*, Seth Holmes (2013) testifies to what it is like to work and live alongside the Triqui Indians as they attempt to cross the border and work in the US fields under physically arduous and exploitative conditions. This inside point of view from the farmworkers themselves captures the particularity and emotional texture of this kind of life in order to defy some assumptions commonly made about migrant farmworkers. First, we see why many Mexicans and indigenous Indians undertake the dangerous and risky border crossing to work in the United States. It is not because they have a choice, but because larger structural conditions create poverty and economic hardship in the Global South. Through Holmes's interviews with Triqui farmworkers we see from the inside what it is like to endure racial insults, unfair pay, and assaults to the humanity and dignity of Triqui workers. This ethnography resists ethical damage by shifting our moral appraisals beyond the localizing blame of individual farmworkers. By Holmes's analysis we newly understand what should be the focus of our moral review: public policy, politics, immigration laws, and larger economic forces. As Holmes (2013, 13) reminds us, migrant farmworkers themselves have no way to influence those laws or institutions that extract the maximum amount of labor for minimal protections in pay, health care, education, or social services.

In *Food Chains* (Longoria and Schlosser 2014) we also see how a food justice narrative challenges oppressive ideologies about migrant farmworkers. In this case the story is told from the point of view of those who pick tomatoes in Immokalee, Florida. Workers testify to exploitative working conditions and labor practices. Included also are the poignant stories of women who endure sexual abuse in the fields with little legal oversight and virtually no recourse to complain. But the ethical lens enables the viewer to achieve the same broad explanatory framework provided by Holmes's ethnography since these injustices are situated within more complicated economic conditions of supply chains. The target of our moral indignation is not necessarily directed at the farmer who employs migrant workers. It is more accurately aimed at a few large corporations, like Publix, who create downward pressure in the buying chain, and consequently disadvantage farmworkers who have the least amount to spare and who are the most politically and economically vulnerable population. The hunger strike undertaken by the Coalition of Immokalee Workers (CIW) supplies the viewer with an emotionally riveting story. In the end the strike does nothing to bring Publix to the table to discuss the Fight for Fair Food initiative. But what the viewer gains is an inspirational model about how to advocate for social and political justice for those who pick our food.

Two food justice narratives are presented as case studies in Chapter 6. In different ways Michael Prager's (2010) memoir *Fat Boy, Thin Man*, and the documentary film *Fed Up* (Soechtig 2014) target what I called the "moral fault narrative." Prager's story challenges the moral fault narrative by describing the lived experience of food addiction. We see from his point of view how control over food choices is compromised in actual settings where the food environment creates obstacles to Prager's recovery. What we newly understand from Prager's poignant testimony is that overcoming a dysfunctional relationship to food is not achieved by "taking more individual responsibility," but by changing the external circumstances or context in order to heal oneself. These conditions include social support by friends and family, therapeutic intervention, and by removing himself entirely from a toxic food environment. Prager's story profiles these background conditions as necessary for understanding the lived experience of obesity.

The moral fault narrative is also challenged by the documentary film, *Fed Up*. Here we are invited into the lives of particular children who struggle with obesity in the context of family, school, exercise routines, and doctor's appointments. Resisting the moral fault narrative is achieved by situating the reader to see how choices about what and how much to eat are shaped by a variety of forces involving cultural norms about weight, lack of knowledge about healthy food, school lunch programs that include mainly processed food, and the ubiquitous sugary drinks and salty snacks on offer in small corner stores and in the aisles of retail grocery stores. These circumstances that contextualize the lived experience of obesity have implications for ascriptions of moral responsibility. By using Vargas's nuanced account of situated agency and responsibility we see that these contextual conditions are crucial for understanding how an agent's capacities for volitional control can be compromised when choices are few and when access to healthy food is limited. One consequence of using and applying Vargas's account of moral responsibility is that it will turn out that many who are obese are not morally responsible for their condition of obesity in a particular set of circumstances because they fail to have the capacity for volitional control in that context. Thus they do not deserve the moral blame that is sometimes attributed to them. But another equally significant result of the account of responsibility used here is that it makes sense to widen the moral lens beyond individuals who are too often depicted as existing in isolation from social, political, and economic contexts. Instead we can point to conditions that create and sustain diminished capacities to detect the moral considerations that favor healthy eating as well as those which compromise capacities for volitional control. What new understanding is achieved by extending the scope of responsibility beyond individuals is a more perspicuous focus on the "moral architecture" of our culture. This refers to conditions that we should intentionally target for change in order to enhance the capacities of morally responsible agents. These background conditions include public health policies, corporate actors that manipulate consumers by marketing and selling foods high in sugar or fat, and disparities of income that create unequal access to health care, housing, and healthy food, to name just a few.

Who does *what* with the story?

I asked one of my contacts at a local hunger relief organization what kinds of obstacles interfered with the goals of doing food justice advocacy work. She had this to say:

> What's been happening here lately is that we realize we need to train staff to identify the root causes of food injustice. So we've been focusing on that. The next, deeper level will be engaging in a new narrative. I would point to our primary challenges as these:
>
> 1. Inertia. Without a *reason* to do things differently, our staff will continue to tell the same stories, especially if they work in getting us donations (which they do).
> 2. Lack of knowledge. Many of our staff and members just don't know about the root causes of food injustice, which is why we've been focusing on that lately.
> 3. Volunteerism. Most people who come to donate or volunteer at … want to feel like they are doing something good, and that whatever action they are taking is making a concrete difference. It's a lot easier to point to a garden or to savings in groceries, than to point to nebulous "food systems change." This is part of why we have shifted to doing policy and organizing work. But even so, it's hard to impact the food system on a local level in a really meaningful way.

Another manager at a national hunger relief organization coordinates volunteer training. When I asked her what unique challenges she had to address in her training programs she replied:

> So far I've seen that sharing a narrative with volunteers has an emotional impact, but there is not the intended behavior change we had hoped for. We screened *A Place at the Table* to a group of college students, and they grabbed onto the characters in the film in a way that let them see hunger in a new way. They couldn't believe that people who work full time still go hungry. But, it was a challenge connecting those narratives to a justice frame rather than a charity frame. We were with the students for a week, but even after that they were more

> inclined to talk about feeding the hungry through a charity model rather than working towards food justice … Charity is something we are all ingrained to praise and do, and food justice can seem a radical idea, even if exciting.

One moral purpose of using a food justice narrative is to create the conditions necessary for citizens to undertake political responsibility for justice (Wilkins 2005). Unfortunately, there is no clear recipe for how to inspire citizens to assume this sort of political responsibility. Specifically, when structural injustice is implicated as part of our ethical analysis of the food system, it is problematic to disentangle the causal conditions that create harmful effects and which operate collectively to disadvantage individuals and subgroups. No one person or collective actor can be blamed for intentionally causing harms (Young 2011, 100).[1]

This creates a difficulty for the food justice activist. Ordinarily we suppose that identifying the causal agent who is responsible and blameworthy for injustice identifies a target for activism. "This is who we hold accountable, and this is what we must change." But structural conditions as explanations for injustice create a nebulous mark for the activist to transform. Individual blame and accountability seem to be the moral appraisals that justify and inspire the activist's work. Without this (moral) garden trellis of support, food justice activism seems like a diffuse agenda that points everywhere and nowhere at the same time. Maybe it is this indistinct target that explains the practical difficulty of transforming volunteers of hunger relief organizations into policy and food justice advocates; the problem described earlier by our nonprofit managers. One answer to this problem is to reconceive of moral blame differently; what Angela Smith (2013) calls "blame as moral protest."

Blame as protest

What is distinctive about Smith's (2013) moral protest account of blame is that it is intended to capture the disposition to protest conduct that is believed to be wrongful or disrespectful to ourselves or others, even in those cases where blame is directed towards people (or circumstances) who are not within reach of sanctioning activities (p. 30). Blame includes taking a stand against this objectionable treatment, signaling that the conduct violates our "basic norms of mutual respect and recognition" (p. 36). The protest part of blame refers to a challenge or repudiation of what is presumed by the wrongdoer; namely, that the person wronged is not deserving of moral respect. Smith formulates the Moral Protest Account in this way:

> To *blame* another is to judge that she is blameworthy (i.e. to judge that she has attitudes that impair her relations with others) and to modify one's own attitudes, intentions, and expectations toward that person as a way of *protesting* (i.e., registering and challenging) the moral claim implicit in her conduct, where such protest implicitly seeks some kind of moral acknowledgment on the part of the blameworthy agent and/or on the part of others in the moral community. (p. 43)

As Smith (2013) describes, it is the first aim that is primary. Even in cases where it is not likely that protesting functions to prompt moral recognition, blaming still operates to register "unjustified disregard shown to a morally considerable being" (p. 43). Understood in this way the practice of blaming is essentially communicative in the sense that it demands moral recognition even if it is not acknowledged by the wrongdoer. This account of blame has some powerful practical applications for the food justice activist.

First, consider how suitable it is for the food justice activist to deploy the blame as protest account. The activist is willing and motivated to make her views public. It is not merely that she is emotionally invested in change. She is also prepared to articulate her convictions about what is right, fair, or just, as well as to draw attention to circumstances that are unjust or morally unacceptable. So in order to bring about change the activist must first *challenge* existing conditions, practices, policies, or laws. But the force of this challenge typically identifies what is underneath these morally suspect practices, policies, or laws; namely, the presumption that the person who is wronged is not deserving of respect. It is the wrongdoer's moral disregard for the person who is wronged that sparks the challenge, and sparks the activist's protest. The activist may specifically target the wrongdoer in order to prompt moral recognition. But even in the absence of any kind of response, the public character of protest signals to a larger constituency (the moral community) that those who are wronged do not deserve such treatment.

But can blame as protest be directed at systemic injustice? Who in these cases is to blame? And what would it mean to "blame the system" as opposed to the kind of being that can be held morally responsible for his or her conduct (Smith 2013, 47)? These questions are answered partly by what Smith has to say about blaming those in the distant past who are not now living. Consider, for example, present blame of those who perpetrated slavery in the United States. In these cases blame does not have the primary aim of seeking moral recognition from those who engaged in wrongdoing, for example, slaveholders, but a secondary aim designed to seek moral recognition from the wider moral community. In this way blame continues to have a "point" even if the wrongdoer does not, or cannot, acknowledge that his behavior is wrong (p. 45).

But, additionally, it is simply too sweeping to maintain that structural conditions cannot be explained by reference to individual people or collectives that contribute in essential ways to creating or sustaining injustice. There are, for example, individual people who create and implement public policy, pass laws or publically resist particular policies. Our moral indignation is correctly directed towards those who are in positions of power to cut food stamp eligibility requirements, decrease aid to dependent children, eliminate funding for "Meals on Wheels," those who voted for stricter and less humane immigration policies, and those corporate decision-makers at Publix who declined to speak with fasting CIW farmworkers. These are legitimate targets of our moral blame because of their respective contributions to creating and sustaining injustice in the food system. And the protest part of this account of blame captures exactly what many food justice narratives profile. Recall the emotional force conveyed when Barbie and others from the organization Witness to Hunger speak poignantly to Congress about what it means to be hungry and have hungry children (*A Place at the Table*). Consider the public demand for moral recognition that the CIW directs to executives at Publix by their hunger strike (*Food Chains*). Or, consider the moral indignation that targets the fast food industry on behalf of overweight children who must navigate the unhealthy foods in their school cafeterias (*Fed Up*). As I write this blame as protest is directed at those in our current US administration who create and seek to implement inhumane and unjust immigration policies. In all of these cases there are indeed many causal factors that contribute to what can still be correctly described as structural injustice. But this explanation of things does not preclude identifying, protesting, challenging, and demanding that individual actors or collectives that contribute to these injustices be held to account. There is every likelihood that such demands will not (always) result in apology, regret, or revisions in the conduct or behavior of those who contribute in primary ways to injustice. But the point of protest in such cases is to publically identify those who *should* change their conduct and to apply social pressure by the wider community for moral recognition. By using an account of moral blame as protest we may situate the food justice activist to correctly target what must change. The activist can focus her critical review on, and challenge, those background conditions that are morally unacceptable, as well as those actors that contribute in a significant way to creating unjust structural conditions.[2]

Do something

There is no one particular thing that I recommend for the food justice activist to do. However, I borrow a few general guidelines from Young's (2011) positive theory about taking responsibility for justice. The *social connection model* of responsibility is forward-looking. First, it describes this kind of responsibility as shared for the following reason. No doubt we each contribute to producing harms created by structures, processes, and institutions. But because we may not be able to disentangle our own individual actions from these structural conditions that create such harms, then we are each responsible for transforming these processes in an effort to reduce injustice. Second, discharging the ordinary citizen's political responsibilities on behalf of food justice involves collective action.[3] This guideline has more to do with pragmatic efficacy since we are individually constrained when acting alone to change "rules, norms, and [the] material effects of structural processes" (pp. 110–12).

My own practical activities are a somewhat imperfect realization of the social connection model of responsibility. Remember that I started out with a backyard garden, and too much kale? I did not start growing vegetables for any ideological reasons. I was just drawn to the task of garden design, and planting particular vegetables because I liked caring for and, ultimately, eating these things. But if you have been following my story between the lines of theoretical analysis, you will notice that having too much kale (basil, chard, or beans), for example, redirected my gaze. You can only give away vegetables to people who actually want or need them. Who are these people? My first idea about this was the local Senior Center, two blocks away. But as I discovered when you start looking around your community for an opportunity to offload vegetables you will get a glimpse of an entire local infrastructure that is devoted to feeding underserved populations. In my community this is the Interfaith Food Shelf, the Joint Council for Economic Opportunity that runs a food shelf, and local church organizations that rotate free meal services throughout five different days of the week. I quickly realized that the need was significantly greater than I could provide by my own extra produce. This was the moment when I began to think not like an individual but like a collective consisting of like-minded gardeners who *each* had too much kale, and the rest. I was delighted to discover that I did not have to start from scratch. There is, in fact, a national organization called Plant a Row for the Hungry (PAR) which is devoted to encouraging local communities to plant and distribute fresh food from backyard gardens and community gardens to underserved populations ("Plant a Row for the Hungry," n.d. *Garden Writers Association*). So what I envisioned was a Plattsburgh chapter of PAR. This quickly escalated to gathering people, advertising, a website, brochures, press releases, and garden signs, all advertising Plattsburgh PAR. I have nothing bad to say about my experiences doing this work for 3–4 years. It was grassroots rewarding but very labor intensive. I met earnest and devoted gardeners who spent many hours transporting and packaging food to various destinations in our community. I got to know cooks and servers at the food shelves and church meal programs who have been steadfast volunteers for decades, long before I even knew there were such programs. And I met many local farmers who eventually discovered that there was someone to call to glean perfectly good squash, turnips, cabbages, and lettuce when these lay unpicked in their fields.

But there was one particular moment that made me pause. I visited our downtown farmer's market at the end of the day in hopes that local farmers would donate their unsold produce to the food shelf. Some of these people were extremely generous and gave me boxes of vegetables. Others told me "no" because they were going to another farmer's market the next day. I suddenly realized (with some degree of shame) that asking for charitable donations from small farmers may be actually cutting into their very precarious profit margins. Instead of asking for vegetable donations, I reasoned that what I should be doing was to find a way to support both the farmers who produce local fresh food, as well as the population of people who have little access to these products. In an instant the charity model that underlies Plattsburgh PAR seemed inadequate to the task. This is how things get complicated because food justice issues are not addressed by charity alone. It is about complex relationships between many interest groups, individual people, organizations, and policies. And Plattsburgh PAR only satisfied one strand of this intricate knot of affiliations. So I was inspired to look around at what other hunger relief agencies were doing. One organization in St. Lawrence County is GardenShare which has a program called "Bonus Bucks" ("Bonus Bucks—Making Local Food Affordable," n.d. *GardenShare*). Visitors to their website are free to donate dollars to this particular program which helps families purchase a Community Supported Agriculture (CSA) share from a nearby farm. In this way the local farmers benefit as well as those people who may not be able to afford to buy fresh seasonal food.

Once food justice objectives come into clear view it is not hard to find already existing organizations that do exactly this kind of work. One of my favorites is WhyHunger, a nonprofit devoted to issues of food insecurity, but one that situates this problem nationally and globally within the complex collection of issues about poverty, social inequality, food sovereignty, and the fundamental right to food. This is not just your ordinary charity organization. A visit to the main page of their website says,

WhyHunger's programs and strategies coalesce around three strategic goals:

1. Movement building—Build and strengthen grassroots-led movements for food justice and food sovereignty worldwide.
2. Social justice—Work for social justice by addressing the root causes of hunger and the deep inequities of poverty at the intersection of economic inequality, racism, health and the environment.
3. Human rights—Work to protect and advance the right to nutritious food for all. ("How We Work," n.d. *WhyHunger*)

The idea that we can and should contribute to collective organizations that address public policy and sustainable approaches to correcting systemic injustices in the food system is neither an original idea, nor a new one. But, I confess, it took me awhile to figure out. My Plattsburgh PAR days may be over, albeit with a lot of extra advertising garden signs stored in the attic. But more recently I have had the opportunity to serve on the Plattsburgh Community Garden Executive Board as well as the Ag Program Committee that serves the regional office of Cornell Cooperative Extension. Both of these committees allowed me a vantage point that is crucial for seeing how local food systems operate here in my own community. With hindsight I see now that my own activities over time have moved from personal initiatives involving growing, preserving, and eating food from my own garden, to participating in collective organizations that potentially allow for justice issues to emerge in making local public policy. In my case this trajectory towards policy work is really more like an accidental consequence than a life lived by design. It is a way of practicing philosophy that takes you by surprise. Happily the stories I have told throughout earlier chapters point in the same direction, like traffic signs that flash yellow or red. The stories alert us to the critical need for food justice activism while at the same time bringing into sharper focus what to target by this activism. So maybe you, the reader, can do better.

Mother Hubbard's Cupboard: Patrick

While I am talking to Erin at her desk, Patrick, my "food bank mentor," is sweeping, singing, and straightening shelves. I can see he is antsy and wants to get going. But he is surprisingly eager to be interviewed to tell me his story. This probably has nothing to do with the joke we shared earlier when I promised to "make him famous" by writing about him…

How did you get started working at the MHC?

Like Erin, Patrick first came to MHC to shop for food.

"It was just such a relief to come here, and everyone greeted me really warmly. I just felt truly welcome."

"I lost my job after about nine years. It was during the economic downturn. But it didn't really affect me like some other people who have a mortgage or children. I just 'circled the wagons' and used the MHC to supplement my food purchases. In addition, I started gardening, built up a seed bank and germinated these seeds to grow things at my house. And, I learned what a complete idiot I had been when I had a job. Now I can buy and cook a chicken, and live off this food for about a week. I used to spend US$ 4 or 5 just on a cup of coffee when I had a job. But that was crazy."

"I just couldn't believe how welcoming everyone was at the food pantry. No one wore uniforms. There didn't seem to be a judgmental attitude from the people who were volunteering. So, I knew right from the start that I wasn't just visiting; I was also going to volunteer here. It's really in my heart to do this kind of service."

What do you like now about what you do? What are the challenges you face?

"Now when I'm helping about two hours a week at MHC it just is a quality bit of my life. I'm getting on my feet a bit more now. I have a goal, and that is to get health insurance. I want to contribute back to society more than I am because I'm just moving off government assistance. I don't consider myself there yet because I don't have insurance. But that's my goal."

So, where do you go from here? What do you imagine yourself doing in the future?

"I'm happiest when I'm the least tied to material things; when everything is simpler. I learned this through experience and not from my family or growing up. For example, when I used to eat at a local free meal house, I felt like a common person and that it is healthy, in a way, to eat alongside street people. The more common people I hang out with, the more normal I feel. And there are a lot of people who need help. There is need everywhere if you just look. Strangely, I think the poorest of the poor have more skills than we do because they need a system to survive. That's something I admire."

"I think I'll be happiest in the future if I end up doing something that lets me give back. When you live a certain way, you automatically take more than your fair share. I feel like I owe something."

So, what advice would you give to young people (or older ones)?

Patrick is a bit reluctant to say what others ought to do or how they ought to live. But after holding his head for a minute or two he says something that will stick with me for quite a while.

"There are a lot of quality futures out there for people. Even a professional life counts as one because society needs people with these skills. But when you hear the expression, 'Walk in somebody else's shoes,' what's important is not to try to get inside another person's feelings exactly."

"I think the only way you can figure out how to live is to actually try to live that way in order to gain experience. Take six months off to see how it feels to give back in some way. And really find out how to do this. Your emotions and your body may speak to you, and then you can make decisions about how to live based on your own heart. Giving back is something that you try. Be a devotee. Have a unique experience."

As I listened to Patrick giving this advice I focused on his earnest expression and steady eye. I wished I could have filmed him making these remarks. This is a person who will shoot baskets at the Food Bank in between loading frozen foods and milk products onto a cart bound for the MHC pantry. He usually arrives on his yellow scooter with a bright green knit hat and flowing lime fluorescent scarf. He laughs easily and makes me feel as if he is immediately my best friend. But when he gives this advice he is speaking with passion about his own life and what gives it meaning. I am on the verge of tears to hear him say these things with so much simple eloquence.

When I say my final goodbyes, Patrick hugs me firmly. "Well, at least we won't have to worry about your car breaking down and you getting home alright" he says, eying my Hyundai Genesis. I am one less person that he needs to help. But in the short time we have spent together Patrick already regards me as someone worthy of concern, I hope. He has certainly won my heart by his honesty, his wonderful sense of fun and good humor, and his deep commitment to helping people who are in need.

Notes

Introduction

1 There are recent anthologies that aim for exactly this kind of broad and comprehensive inclusion of topics about food and ethics. See, for example, Barnhill, Doggett, and Budolfson (2016, 2018); Alkon and Agyeman (2011).

2 See, for example, Blum (1994, 43).

3 Nelson (2001, 42) describes an example where a person, Billy, undertakes to read romantic novels as a way to inform himself about how to treat a future soulmate. This is a case where Billy may fail to have both narrative competence and normative competence (originally introduced in DePaul 1993).

4 Admittedly, some of these narratives recognize the limitations on choice that I want to talk about. For example, *Food Fight* (Taylor 2008) includes an interview with Will Allen who works to bring fresh food to low-income families in Milwaukie, Wisconsin.

5 Nelson (2001, 168) also describes a damaging master narrative as one that is "[silent] about the conditions under which people actually live their lives."

6 Nelson (2001, 7) says that a counterstory corrects for the way in which master narratives "misrepresent persons and situations." Abstracting from particular identities of food consumers may certainly skew our grasp of what kind of social change or public policy is needed to improve access to nutritious food, even if this is not a case of "misrepresentation."

7 See also "About Us," n.d. *Food First.*

1 Ethical Perception

1 See T. H. Irwin (2000) for an interpretation of Aristotle on this point. Further discussion of "moral particularism" can be found in Little and Hooker (2000). Giving conceptual priority to the particular is not an original thesis. See also Pritchard (1996), Nussbaum (1990), and Garfield (2000).

2 Aristotle (*NE* 1142a23) says:

> Practical wisdom is of the ultimate and particular, of which there is no scientific understanding, but a kind of perception—not, I mean, ordinary sense-perception of the proper objects of each sense, but the sort of

perception by which we grasp that a certain figure is composed in a certain way out of triangles.

3 Blum (1994, 46) disagrees with Nussbaum on this point.

4 This example varies slightly from one described by Blum (1994, 31–4).

5 For example, see Novella Carpenter's (2017) immensely popular blog about Ghost Town Farm. See also the "how to" guide to urban farming by Carpenter and Rosenthal (2011).

6 Misak (2008, 631) adds the following questions to judge and evaluate the narrator's account:

> In addition to the considerations articulated thus far, we will likely want to include what follows. Does the narrator seem boastful, vain, or self-indulgent, or does he seem focused on wanting to tell a good (perhaps lively, entertaining, or scary) story as opposed to wanting to tell an accurate story? Is there evidence of wishful thinking, bitterness, or external motivations such as ideology, nostalgia, patriotism, or self-hatred? Do the events recounted fit with the known facts? Are the lessons drawn from the experiences such that they resonate with others who have had similar experiences? Are the purported moral insights such that they clash or cohere with other moral insights? Are those lessons and insights well supported by other arguments, or are there powerful arguments which run counter to them?

7 We might also use additional readings to supply the critical review of a narrative. For example, one might pair a reading of *Farm City* together with McClintock (2011). In his study of the flatlands of Oakland, McClintock describes the historical processes that created this "almost entirely treeless and worn landscape of used car dealerships, taco trucks, liquor stores, dilapidated storefronts, and the occasional chain linked vacant lot" (p. 91). McClintock documents a combination of factors at work over time that eventually resulted in restricted access to healthy food for residents of West Oakland, and unevenly developed the city's landscape. These include: industrial location, residential development, city planning, and racist mortgage lending (redlining). He calls the structural forces that operated historically on this area, "demarcated devaluation"—a kind of devaluing of capital that targets a geographical location and its residents.

8 See also Nussbaum (1990, 54–105).

9 Robinson's (2005) overall project involves characterizing what emotions are in such a way as to explain their role in literature, art, and music. Generally she characterizes an episode of emotion as a "process, consisting minimally in a non-cognitive affective appraisal succeeded by physiological changes of specific sorts, action tendencies, and cognitive monitoring of the non-cognitive affective appraisal and the other elements of the response" (p. 157). The precise details of this definition of emotion will not change the primary use I make of Robinson's proposal about

how narratives can be instructive in guiding readers' emotions in making ethical judgments about real-world situations and people.

10 These initiatives were, in part, a response to a fractured community, reeling from the 1992 riots after the acquittal of those responsible for the beating of Rodney King.

11 The city purchased the property from Horowitz in 1986 for $5 million, and sold it back to Horowitz in 2002 for $5 million. The estimated loss to the taxpayers was $10–15 million.

12 Also militating against this ethical position is the suggestion made in the film that the city was engaged in a "back room deal" when they sold this property back to Horowitz.

2 Developing Narrative Skill

1 See, for example, the approach used to teach character education in New York state called Positive Behavioral Interventions and Supports ("PBIS in the Classroom," 2017).

2 See also Annas (1995), Homiak (2004), and Swartwood (2012).

3 See, in particular, the following discussions of moral particularism: Garfield (2000), Lance and Little (2004, 2006), and Little (2000, 2001b, 2007).

4 Arguably, learning how to drive is more like learning how to ride a bike than learning how to play chess. In both driving and biking the activity is not governed by a prescriptive rule that the learner follows. It is the experience that matters; the feel of balancing over a bumpy road, leaning into a turn, and so on, that makes the novice bike rider into an expert. Similarly, a novice car driver does get better and better as she gains experiences in varied driving conditions, but this expertise is not owed to any kind of rule or maxim even in the initial stages of driving, contrary to what Dreyfus and Dreyfus say.

5 For a detailed discussion of the variety of circumstances surrounding the appropriateness of laughter and humor, see Bakhurst (2008).

6 When moral particularists refer to the uncodifiability of moral generalities, what they mean is that there are no finitely specifiable necessary and sufficient conditions linking moral and non-moral properties. For example, if Lisa is cruel, then she might be so by virtue of any number of facts about her thinking, saying, or doing. She might be cruel by insulting her teacher, teasing a friend who is sensitive, not inviting a member of her class to a party, causing pain by kicking a dog, or permitting a dog that is in pain to continue to live, and so on. The non-naturalist will argue that there is no useful way of specifying the conditional, "If M, then N" where "M" is any moral property and "N" is any non-moral property.

The more radical moral particularist argument about context implies that there is no useful, finitely specifiable conditional of the form, "If N, then M." Here the illustrative examples suggest that even the presence of typical good-making properties like pleasure, and typical bad-making properties like pain, when embedded in certain kinds of contextual circumstances, will not imply their predictable moral valence. The pleasure felt by the student who performs community service may be a good in this particular case, but the pleasure experienced by the sadist who tortures, contributes essentially to its moral wrongness. The way in which pleasure contributes to the other contextual features in each case can switch the moral valence or evaluation of the act performed. This is sometimes referred to as "holism" with respect to moral reasons. Similarly, we might say that a stripe of red paint in one composition makes a painting aesthetically good. But the contribution that this particular brush stroke makes in one painting does not necessarily carry over to other paintings. Adding the same stripe of color to another painting might create an aesthetically awful creation. Its aesthetic goodness or badness depends on all of its features, taken together, in the same way that all of the contextual non-moral features (including pleasure or pain) taken together contribute to its moral status. One way of putting this point is to say that the moral domain is "shapeless with respect to the non-moral." For accounts of moral particularism see, for example, Dancy (2004); and selections from Hooker and Little (2000).

7 See also Little (2000).

8 For other similar descriptions of the use of paradigms in ethical reasoning see (Matthews 1994) and Pritchard (1996).

9 Little (2000, 297) describes the idea of epistemic skills in the following way:

> What it takes to make judgments of justification are, broadly put, epistemic *skills.* It is a skill to read the world—to know what, in the face of an infinite amount of change, would for a given purpose count as a sufficiently relevantly similar world, to know when a pattern is robust, to know how to navigate through patterns of competing influences, to determine which possibilities are epistemically relevant alternatives, to know when you know enough and when you don't, to know when you have entered a context in which previous experience no longer points the way. Such skills, like any others, are not exhausted by knowledge of some codifiable set of propositions (think of knowing how to drive): knowing how, as the saying goes, cannot be reduced to knowing that ... We make judgments here, then, as we do anywhere—by consulting our experience of patterns and our sense of current conditions, and invoking our competency with the relevant epistemological concepts such as *relevance, robustness, similarity.*

10 Little (2000, 173) remarks,

> A heuristic, after all, is a technique for getting someone to see or interpret a situation in a certain way, akin to turning one's head sideways to see the duck

in the duck-rabbit figure—something that, to work, need not be a proposition, much less a true one.

11 The assumption that the ethical novice relies on ethical rules initially is made by a number of philosophers who endorse a skill model of virtue. See, for example, Dreyfus and Dreyfus (2004), Stichter (2007, 2011), and Jacobson (2005).

12 A delightful and illustrative example of this way of reasoning occurs in *Honest Andrew* (Skurzynski 1980). Andrew finds himself in an awkward position at the dinner table when his mother serves crayfish. Andrew *hates* crayfish but, not wanting to hurt her feelings, he stuffs the crayfish into the sides of his cheeks and then sneaks outside to deposit these so he can help himself to dessert. His father catches him in this deceit and takes the opportunity to instruct his son about the "Otter Motto" that has guided otter behavior throughout history—"Always tell the truth." Very quickly we see how this general rule admits of a variety of exceptions, to the dismay of Andrew's mother. Andrew proceeds to explain, in excruciating detail, how he feels when he is greeted by Professor Otter and asked, "How are you?" He honestly tells his woodchuck neighbor that her baby is not pretty when asked, "Isn't she darling?" And he honestly corrects (and "sasses") his Aunt Prissy Porcupine when she remarks that he is a "big otter." In all these cases we see that the Otter Motto "Tell the Truth" fails to usefully incorporate the contextual details about conversational etiquette, hurt feelings, and respecting your elders. Andrew and his father manage to revise the Otter Motto to become, "Always tell the truth, but be as nice and polite about it as one can." Interestingly, the story begins with Andrew exhibiting sensitivity to the circumstances of his truth-telling when he quietly disposes of his crayfish dinner. It is Andrew's father who must learn to *see* that the Otter Motto admits of exceptions.

According to Pritchard (1996), these kinds of contextual details in the story do not invite children to be skeptical about truth-telling. Rather, he suggests that what we might take from this story is the idea that there are sometimes other values at stake (consideration, politeness) in addition to truth-telling that we must take into account on particular occasions. Nonetheless, one might suspect that there is something else at stake here as well—the plausibility of the general rule itself. Even though Andrew employs the revised Otter Motto to better effect when his mother serves him Salamander Stew (he politely declines his share of stew), there is still little hope that this revised general rule, "Always tell the truth, but be as nice and polite about it as one can," will stand. For there are many other contexts where one ought not to tell the truth—to protect a friend from harm, to spare a child the complicated details of a divorce, etc. The general revised rule about truth-telling may not survive this onslaught of contextual details about person, place, time, intention, or consequences, among other features. Or, at least, the revised rule may fail to be helpfully action-guiding (Dunn 1999).

13 See, for example, Coyle (2009).

14 See, for example, the "Discussion Plans and Exercises" in the teacher's manual to accompany *Nous* (Lipman 1996b, 3, 8–9, 130).

15 But rules are not ignored altogether in *Nous* or in the accompanying teacher's manual, *Deciding What to Do* (Lipman 1996b, 100). When Ms. Merle teaches her students the virtues, she employs rules as one of her methods. Nonetheless, the issue about whether or not this is a good methodology for moral education is up for review, by the characters in *Nous* as well as by the children reading the novel. See Leading Idea 2: Ms. Merle's method of moral instruction.

16 Lobel (1980, 38).

17 Coincidentally, this story fits one of Aristotle's virtues like a glove. The classical conception of the virtue of temperance is concerned with bodily pleasures of touch and taste; specifically, the bodily appetites of eating, drinking, and sexual activity (*NE* 1118b1–5). Some appetites are considered "natural," such as an appetite for nourishment in humans as well as an appetite for sex in young people. But as with all the virtues we are in danger of erring by committing the vice of excess or the vice of deficiency relative to the mean state of the virtue of temperance. These are referred to respectively as "gluttony" and "insensibility." If a person is intemperate by committing vices of excess, he may err in a number of different ways. Aristotle (*NE* 1118b25) says that such a person may:

(i) "enjoy the wrong things," or things that are "hateful";
(ii) Enjoy some things in excess or considerably more than others do; or
(iii) Enjoy some things in the wrong way.

In our story Hippo clearly commits the vice of excess in the sense of (ii) by consuming more food than he ought. Even though it is a natural desire to nourish oneself, Hippo exceeds what he needs to nourish himself. Aristotle remarks that the intemperate person has an appetite for all pleasant things and chooses these at the cost of everything else. Moreover, he feels pain when he fails to get something for which he has a keen appetite (*NE* 11199). Recall how annoyed Hippo is when he fails to get the desired (huge) proportions of brussels sprouts, mashed potatoes, and bean soup!

3 Food Insecurity: Hungry Women

1 Poppendieck (1998, 188–9) notes that many of the people who participate in charitable food programs are motivated to do so for religious beliefs. She remarks, "The emergency food system is permeated with religion. More than 70 percent of the pantries and kitchens affiliated with the Second Harvest Network are sponsored by churches or other religious organizations."

2 See also Egan (2017) in the *New York Times* editorial, "The Deserving Rich and the Deserving Poor." Egan characterizes recent political debates about children's health that target the poor as narrative "fictions."

3 Not all the stories that fit this paradigm are about women. Consider the following story about Marvin, a fifty-one-year-old Georgia resident, whose story begins with his loss of hearing as a child, and the gradual loss of his vision as an adult. Devoted to finding work even though he does not see well, he is forced to seek menial labor such as washing windows or mowing lawns. But then he is hit by a car, and now he is unable to work at all, though he still strongly desires to do so. Marvin hopes that he will eventually "get back on his feet." In the meantime he is grateful for receiving food stamps because they keep him from going hungry.

Like the other stories I profile about "hungry women," Marvin's story elicits sympathy from us largely because it is about how bad luck can bring a person down. Significantly, the conditions that impede Marvin from working are illnesses and accidents for which he is not to be blamed. This allows us to see him as an agent who has all the right motivational states for living a better life: he *wants* to work. But at the same time his actions are constrained by circumstances out of his control. His inability to work and thus to feed himself is shaped by these contingencies. The reader of this story senses that if life had dealt Marvin a slightly different hand, then he would surely make good on his responsibility to provide food for himself.

4 Meyers characterizes this kind of problem as a dilemma that confronts how we shape efforts to eradicate global poverty. "The dilemma arises when we ask who is to decide or how these [choices about how to live, aspects of material and emotional well-being, and capabilities to function] are to be defined, and what are to be taken as the goods to be secured and the bads to be avoided." My criticism of the storytelling project employed by GlobalGiving suggests that we err in the direction of one horn of the dilemma by allowing those individuals who are food-insecure to articulate the problems and standards for alleviating their needs. As Meyers suggests, these standards may be set by "circumscribed experiences" or a "stunted vision of what is possible" (Meyers 2014). See also Card (2014) and Cudd (2014).

4 Rewriting the Call to Charity

1 On a similar theme, Poppendieck (1998, 19) describes the "[King] Wenceslas syndrome" in the following way:

> The process by which the joys and demands of personal charity divert us from more fundamental solutions to the problems of deepening poverty and growing inequality, and the corresponding process by which the diversion

of our efforts leaves the way wide open to those who want more inequality, not less.

2 At times Kelly (2013, 256) suggests that compassion is the appropriate response to judgments about unfair burdens that make it difficult for a person to meet moral expectations. In this description the judgment about unfairness comes first, and compassion follows. But elsewhere Kelly remarks that when we are privy to descriptions of scenarios that create difficult obstacles to acting responsibly, these scenarios "trigger" our compassion. And it is this emotional response that leads to judgments that there exist mitigating moral excuses. Either description of the causal role of compassion on Kelly's account locates this emotional response at the center of our blaming practice, not as a moral requirement, but as a signal that even though a person may have acted wrongly our blame is misdirected.

3 The mission of the organization is described in the following way:

> Our programs in 24,000 communities throughout Africa, South Asia and Latin America are based on an innovative, holistic approach, which empowers women and men living in rural villages to become the agents of their own development and make sustainable progress in overcoming hunger and poverty. ("Who We Are," n.d. *The Hunger Project*)

4 See "Stories of Success," n.d. *The Hunger Project*.

5 See "Issues," n.d. *The Hunger Project*.

5 Farmworkers: "It is Very Ugly Here"

1 See, in particular, the following description of master narratives by Nelson (2001, 162):

> Some master narratives hide the existence of coercion by *naturalizing* an oppressive identity. Naturalizing an identity is a matter of making it seem inevitable that certain groups of peoples must occupy certain places in society.

2 See also Bardacke (2011), "The Work Itself," pp. 30–42.

3 For facts about farmworker health see "Farmworker Fact Sheets," n.d. *National Center for Farmworker Health*.

4 For another excellent example of this inside point of view, see Nazario (2006).

5 Perhaps some of the most pernicious examples of false narratives about immigrants come from US President Trump who has stated that, "When Mexico sends its people … They're bringing drugs. They're bringing crime. They're rapists." See Beinart (2017).

6 For a thorough and riveting account of abuses in tomato agriculture, see Estabrook (2011).

7 For a description of the concept of being powerless see Nelson (2001, 110).

8 See also Bardacke (2011), Garcia (2012), and Shaw (2008).

9 For practical suggestions to implement farmworker justice, see especially the conclusion of Holmes (2013), "Conclusion: Change, Pragmatic Solidarity, and Beyond," pp. 182–98.

6 Obesity, Responsibility, and Situated Agency

1 Identifying obesity as a "problem" (trend or epidemic) is itself contestable. See, for example, Lyons (2009), Guthman (2011), and Kirkland (2011).

2 In *Responsibility for Justice*, Young (2011, 17) makes a similar comment when she discusses personal responsibility in the context of public policy discourse about poverty and welfare reform. She criticizes Charles Murray (1984) and Lawrence Mead (2006) for assuming that individual responsibility and structural explanations of poverty are mutually exclusive explanations. Here I do not charge any one author with the same kind of mistake. What is still problematic is that emphasizing structural conditions in causal accounts of obesity risks understating or neglecting individual agency which most of us believe continues to operate even when choices and opportunities are limited.

3 For example, consider what Congressman Ric Keller says in defense of the Personal Responsibility in Food Consumption Act.

> We believe there should be common sense in a food court, not blaming other people in a legal court whenever there is an excessive consumption of fast food … We think that most people understand that its common sense that if you eat unlimited amounts of supersize fries and milkshakes and Big Macs … that can possibly lead to obesity and things like diabetes [and] cardiovascular disease. (As quoted in Benfarado, Hanson, and Yosifon 2004)

4 An additional rationale for seeking clarity about obesity and moral responsibility is that some kinds of obesity prevention policy recommendations may depend on targeting those populations of people who are believed to freely and knowingly undertake risks with their health. See, for example, the discussion of fairness in (Wikler 1987; Knowles 1977; Crawford 1977, 1980; Veatch 1980).

5 See, for example, Zinczenko (2002).

6 The theory is "revisionist" in the sense that it requires relinquishing some common sense intuitions about responsibility. See Vargas (2013a, 2).

7 With some variation the following views may qualify as *reasons* accounts: Wolf (1990); Wallace (1994); Fischer and Ravizza (1998); Arpaly (2003); Nelkin (2008). See also Strawson (1962).

8 See also Vargas's (2013a, 135–57) motivations for adopting a reasons account.

9 For a more complete explanation of the standard features of reasons accounts that Vargas rejects (atomism and monism), see Vargas (2013a, 204–9).

10 Following Ciurria (2015) we might classify Vargas's account as "psychological externalism" about moral responsibility.

11 Vargas (2013a, 213–14) states this in the following way: "An agent *S* is a responsible agent with respect to considerations of type *M* in circumstances *C* if *S* possesses a suite of basic agential capacities implicated in effective self-directed agency (including, for example, beliefs, desires, intentions, instrumental reasoning, and generally reliable beliefs about the world and the consequences of action) and is also possessed of the relevant capacity for (A) detection of suitable moral considerations *M* in *C* and (B) self-governance with respect to *M* in *C*."

12 Perhaps she has read Schlosser (2005).

13 Vargas (2013a, 222–3) specifies the conditions for this capacity in the following way:

> The capacity for volitional control, or self-governance with respect to the relevant moral considerations *M* in circumstances *C* obtains when either:
>
> i. *S* is, in light of awareness of *M* in *C*, motivated to accordingly pursue courses of action for which *M* counts in favor, and to avoid courses of action disfavored by *M*; or
> ii. When *S* is not so motivated, in a suitable proportion of those worlds where *S* is in a context relevantly similar to *C*
>   a. *S* detects moral considerations of type *M*, and
>   b. in virtue of detecting *M* considerations, *S* acquires the motivation to act accordingly, and
>   c. *S* successfully acts accordingly.

14 In order to keep this *basic* illustrative example relatively uncomplicated, I do not include a discussion about whether or not Alex is blameworthy for her action.

15 For more philosophical background about addiction and responsibility see Poland and Graham (2011).

16 That is, "the best of reasons cannot compete with the imminent pleasure, comfort, and/or escape they are expecting to experience" (Garrett 2011, 253).

17 See especially Levy (2011) and Charland (2013).

18 This is consistent with how Vargas (2013a, 218–19) explains judgments about similarity of contexts.

19 See also Flanagan (2011) and Hanninen and Koski-Jannes (1999).

20 For more discussion of external constraints on choice see Dixon (2018).

21 See, in particular, a finding of a recent study done by the USDA ("Foods Typically Purchased by Supplemental Nutrition Assistance Program (SNAP) Households," November 18, 2016). According to this study, SNAP recipients spent 20 cents on every dollar on the category of junk food including, "sweetened beverages, desserts, salty snacks, candy and sugar." This USDA study of the shopping cart of those who receive food stamps is typical of households in general, making soft drinks

and other sugary beverages the number one purchase. Marion Nestle describes this as a "multibillion-dollar taxpayer subsidy of the soda industry" (as quoted in O'Connor 2017).

22 For more about the "obesogenic environment" see Hill and Peters (1998), Winson (2004), and Guthman (2011). See also Wansik (2004, 2006).

23 In this case the function of moral blame will be different than it is when directed to individual moral agents since, as Vargas (2013a, 243) remarks, institutions and collectives do not have "our ordinary capacities to recognize and respond to moral considerations."

24 Vargas (2013a, 246–7).

25 Vargas (2013a, 246) is sympathetic to using narratives in this way. He says,

> *How* we conceive of our agency, and the powers we take agents to ordinarily have, will play some role in whether or not we are responsible agents in a given context, because of the power of such narratives to structure our agency. By promulgating narratives of control in those circumstances that test our control, we might (at least sometimes) make it the case that agents come to have enough self-control to be responsible agents. Similarly, by promulgating narratives of incapacity, of the inevitability of caving in to nigh-irresistible desires and temptations, we run the risk of self-fulfilling narratives here too.

As we have seen throughout, the possible worries about narratives used in this way to shape agency is that some narratives may have built into them gender, racial, or class stereotypes that degrade individuals and their group identities.

7 Practicing Philosophy

1 Gilson (2014) echoes exactly this concern in writing about the food system.

2 Young (2011, 109) would agree with some of what I say here about identifying structural conditions that contribute to injustice, though she does not share the account of blame as protest that I apply to these conditions. She remarks,

> Understanding how structural processes produce and reproduce injustice requires having an account of how they have come about and operated in the past coming up to the present. Having such a backward-looking account also helps those of us who participate in those processes understand our role in them. The purpose of such backward-looking account, however, is not to praise or to blame, but to help all of us see relationships between particular actions, practices, and policies, on the one hand, and structural outcomes, on the other.

3 See especially Reynolds and Cohen (2016).

References

"About Us." n.d. *Food First*. https://foodfirst.org/about-us/.

"About Us." n.d. *GlobalGiving*. www.globalgiving.org/aboutus/.

Alkon, Alison Hope, and Julian Agyeman, eds. 2011. *Cultivating Food Justice: Race, Class, and Sustainability*. Food, Health, and the Environment. Cambridge, MA: MIT Press.

Allen, Patricia. 2010. "Realizing Justice in Local Food Systems." *Cambridge Journal of Regions, Economy and Society* 3 (2): 295–308.

Allen, Patricia, and Julie Guthman. 2006. "From 'Old School' to 'Farm-to-School': Neoliberalization from the Ground Up." *Agriculture and Human Values* 23 (4): 401–15.

Annas, Julia. 1995. "Virtue as a Skill." *International Journal of Philosophical Studies* 3 (2): 227–43.

Aristotle. 1999. *Nicomachean Ethics*. Translated by Terence Irwin. Second edition. Indianapolis: Hackett.

Arpaly, Nomy. 2003. *Unprincipled Virtue: An Inquiry into Moral Agency*. New York: Oxford University Press.

Ashton, Alison. 2016. "The Temptation Busters." *Parade Magazine*, January 3.

Bakhurst, David. 2008. "Laughter and Moral Ambiguity: Particularist Reflections on the Ethical Dimensions of Humour." In *Challenging Moral Particularism*, edited by Mark Norris Lance, Matjaz Potrc, and Vojko Strahovnik, 192–208. Routledge Studies in Ethics and Moral Theory. New York: Routledge.

Bardacke, Frank. 2011. *Trampling Out the Vintage: Cesar Chavez and the Two Souls of the United Farm Workers*. London: Verso.

Barnhill, Anne, Tyler Doggett, and Mark Budolfson, eds. 2016. *Food, Ethics, and Society: An Introductory Text with Readings*. Oxford: Oxford University Press.

Barnhill, Anne, Tyler Doggett, and Mark Budolfson, eds. 2018. *Oxford Handbook of Food Ethics*. Oxford: Oxford University Press.

Bates, Robert. 2009. *Ingredients*. Documentary. Optic Nerve Productions.

Beinart, Peter. 2017. "Trump Scapegoats Unauthorized Immigrants for Crime." *The Atlantic*, March 1, sec. "Politics."

Benfarado, Adam, Jon Hanson, and David Yosifon. 2004. "Broken Scales: Obesity and Justice in America." *Emory Law Journal* 53 (October): 1645–806.

Berry, Wendell. 2009. *Bringing It to the Table: On Farming and Food*. Berkeley: Counter Point Press.

Bloomfield, Paul. 2000. "Virtue Epistemology and the Epistemology of Virtue." *Philosophy and Phenomenological Research* 60 (1): 23–43.

Bloomfield, Paul. 2001. *Moral Reality*. New York: Oxford University Press.

Blum, Lawrence A. 1994. *Moral Perception and Particularity*. Cambridge: Cambridge University Press.

"Bonus Bucks—Making Local Food Affordable." n.d. *GardenShare*. www.gardenshare.org/content/bonus-bucks-making-local-food-affordable.

Boss, Susie. 2011. "Amplifying Local Voices." *Stanford Social Innovation Review* (Summer). https://ssir.org/articles/entry/amplifying_local_voices1.

Bread for the World. www.bread.org/.

Brighouse, Harry. 2004. *Justice*. Cambridge: Polity Press.

Brownell, Kelly D., and Katherine Battle Horgen. 2004. *Food Fight: The Inside Story of the Food Industry, America's Obesity Crisis, and What We Can Do about It*. New York: McGraw-Hill.

Brownell, Kelly D., and Kenneth E. Warner. 2009. "The Perils of Ignoring History: Big Tobacco Played Dirty and Millions Died. How Similar Is Big Food?" *Millbank Quarterly* 87 (1): 259–94.

Brownell, Kelly D., Rogan Kersh, David S. Ludwig, Robert C. Post, Rebecca M. Puhl, Marlene B. Schwartz, and Walter C. Willett. 2010. "Personal Responsibility and Obesity: A Constructive Approach to a Controversial Issue." *Health Affairs* 29 (3): 378–86.

Card, Claudia. 2014. "Surviving Poverty." In *Poverty, Agency, and Human Rights*, edited by Diana Tietjens Meyers, 21–42. Oxford: Oxford University Press.

Carpenter, Novella. 2009. *Farm City: The Education of an Urban Farmer*. New York: Penguin Books.

Carpenter, Novella. 2017. "Ghost Town Farm." *Ghost Town Farm: A Blog* (April 24). https://ghosttownfarm.wordpress.com/.

Carpenter, Novella, and Willow Rosenthal. 2011. *The Essential Urban Farmer*. New York: Penguin Books.

Charland, Louis C. 2013. "Decision-Making Capacity and Responsibility in Addiction." In *Addiction and Responsibility*, edited by Jeffrey Poland and George Graham, 139–58. Philosophical Psychopathology: Disorders of the Mind. Cambridge, MA: MIT Press.

"Cheers and Jeers." 2014. *Press-Republican*, November 24, sec. "Editorial."

Ciurria, Michelle. 2015. "Moral Responsibility Ain't Just in the Head." *Journal of the American Philosophical Association* 1 (4): 601–16.

Code, Lorraine. 1987. *Epistemic Responsibility*. Hanover, New Hampshire: University Press of New England.

Coyle, Daniel. 2009. *The Talent Code: Greatness Isn't Born. It's Grown. Here's How*. New York: Bantam Books.

Crawford, Robert. 1977. "You Are Dangerous to Your Health: The Ideology and Politics of Victim Blaming." *International Journal of Health Services* 7 (4): 663–80.

Crawford, Robert. 1980. "Healthism and the Medicalization of Everyday Life." *International Journal of Health Services* 10 (3): 365–88.

Cudd, Ann E. 2014. "Agency and Intervention: How (Not) to Fight Global Poverty." In *Poverty, Agency, and Human Rights*, edited by Diana Meyers, 197–222. Oxford: Oxford University Press.

Dancy, Jonathan. 2004. *Ethics Without Principles*. Oxford: Clarendon Press.

"Declaration of Nyeleni." 2007. *Nyeleni 2007*. https://nyeleni.org/spip.php?article290.

DePaul, Michael. 1993. *Balance and Refinement: Beyond Coherence Methods of Moral Inquiry*. London: Routledge.

Dixon, Beth. 2016. "Book Review. The Self-Help Myth: How Philanthropy Fails to Alleviate Poverty." *Journal of Children & Poverty* 22 (1): 68–9.

Dixon, Beth. 2018. "Obesity and Responsibility." In *Oxford Handbook of Food Ethics*, edited by Anne Barnhill, Mark Budolfson, and Tyler Doggett, 614–33. Oxford: Oxford University Press.

Dreyfus, Hubert, and Dreyfus, Stuart. 1991. "Towards a Phenomenology of Ethical Expertise." *Human Studies* 14: 229–50.

Dreyfus, Hubert, and Dreyfus, Stuart. 2004. "The Ethical Implications of the Five-Stage Skill-Acquisition Model." *Bulletin of Science, Technology & Society* 24 (3): 251–64.

Dunn, Allen. 1999. "The Limits of Particularism in the Ethical Criticism of the Novel." *Proceedings of the American Society for Aesthetics*, Pacific Division Annual Meeting.

Egan, Timothy. 2017. "The Deserving Rich and the Deserving Poor." *New York Times*, December 16, sec. "Opinion."

Estabrook, Barry. 2011. *Tomatoland: How Modern Industrial Agriculture Destroyed Our Most Alluring Fruit*. Kansas City, MO: Andrews McMeel.

"Fair Food Program." n.d. *Coalition of Immokalee Workers*. www.ciw-online.org/.

"Farmworker Fact Sheets." n.d. *National Center for Farmworker Health*. www.ncfh.org.

Fischer, John Martin, and Mark Ravizza. 1998. *Responsibility and Control: A Theory of Moral Responsibility*. Cambridge Studies in Philosophy and Law. Cambridge: Cambridge University Press.

Flanagan, Owen. 2011. "What Is It like to Be an Addict?" In *Addiction and Responsibility*, edited by Jeffrey Poland and George Graham, 269–92. Philosophical Psychopathology: Disorders of the Mind. Cambridge, MA: MIT Press.

Food Research and Action Center. http://frac.org/.

"Foods Typically Purchased by Supplemental Nutrition Assistance Program (SNAP) Households." November 18, 2016. *USDA*. www.fns.usda.gov/snap/foods-typically-purchased-supplemental-nutrition-assistance-program-snap-households.

Fraser, Nancy. 1998. "Social Justice in the Age of Identity Politics: Redistribution, Recognition, and Participation." In *The Tanner Lectures on Human Values*, vol. 19, edited by Grethe B. Peterson. Salt Lake City: University of Utah Press.

Frye, Marilyn. 1983. *The Politics of Reality: Essays on Feminist Theory*. Freedom, CA: Crossing Press.

Garcia, Matt. 2012. *From the Jaws of Victory: The Triumph and Tragedy of Cesar Chavez and the Farm Worker Movement*. Berkeley: University of California Press.

Garfield, Jay. 2000. "Particularity and Principle." In *Moral Particularism*, edited by Brad Hooker and Margaret Little, 178–204. Oxford: Clarendon Press.

Garrett, Richard. 2011. "Addiction, Paradox, and the Good I Would." In *Addiction and Responsibility*, edited by Jeffrey Poland and George Graham, 247–68. Philosophical Psychopathology: Disorders of the Mind. Cambridge, MA: MIT Press.

Geneske, Jay. n.d. "Digital Storytelling for Social Impact." *The Rockefeller Foundation*. www.rockefellerfoundation.org/blog/digital-storytelling-social-impact/.

Gilson, Erinn. 2014. "Vote with Your Fork? Responsibility for Food Justice," edited by Jeff Gauthier. *Social Philosophy Today: Food* 30: 113–30.

Goldie, Peter. 2003. "Narrative, Emotion, and Perspective." In *Imagination, Philosophy, and the Arts*, edited by Matthew Kieran and Dominic McIver Lopes, 54–68. London: Routledge.

Gottlieb, Robert, and Anupama Joshi. 2010. *Food Justice*. Food, Health, and the Environment. Cambridge, MA: MIT Press.

Guthman, Julie. 2008. "Bringing Good Food to Others: Investigating the Subjects of Alternative Food Practice." *Cultural Geographies* 15 (4): 431–47.

Guthman, Julie. 2011. *Weighing In: Obesity, Food Justice, and the Limits of Capitalism*. California Studies in Food and Culture. Berkeley: University of California Press.

Hanninen, Vilma, and Anja Koski-Jannes. 1999. "Narratives of Recovery from Addictive Behaviours." *Addiction* 94 (12): 1837–48.

Hassanein, Neva. 2003. "Practicing Food Democracy: A Pragmatic Politics of Transformation." *Journal of Rural Studies* 19 (1): 77–86.

Hill, James O., and John C. Peters. 1998. "Environmental Contributions to the Obesity Epidemic." *Science* 280: 1371–74.

Holmes, Seth M. 2013. *Fresh Fruit, Broken Bodies: Migrant Farmworkers in the United States*. Callifornia Series in Public Anthropology. Berkeley: University of California Press.

Holt-Giménez, Eric. 2011a. *Food Movements Unite!* Oakland, CA: Food First Books.

Holt-Giménez, Eric. 2011b. "Food Security, Food Justice, or Food Sovereignty? Crises, Food Movements, and Regime Change." In *Cultivating Food Justice: Race, Class, and Sustainability*, edited by Alison Hope Alkon and Julian Agyeman, 309–30. Food, Health, and the Environment. Cambridge, MA: MIT Press.

Homiak, Marcia. 2004. "Virtue and the Skills of Ordinary Life." In *Setting the Moral Compass: Essays by Women Philosophers*, edited by Cheshire Calhoun, 23–42. Oxford: Oxford University Press.

"How We Work." n.d. *WhyHunger*. https://whyhunger.org/how-we-work/.

"Hunger in Your Community: Real Stories." n.d. *Feeding America*. www.feedingamerica.org/hunger-in-america/hunger-stories/your-stories/.

Hutchinson, D. S. 1988. "Doctrines of the Mean and the Debate Concerning Skills in Fourth-Century Medicine, Rhetoric and Ethics." *Apeiron* 21 (2): 17–50.

Ingram, David. 2014. "Poverty Knowledge, Coercion, and Social Rights: A Discourse Ethical Contribution to Social Epistemology." In *Poverty, Agency, and Human Rights*, edited by Diana Tietjens Meyers, 43–67. Oxford: Oxford University Press.

Irwin, Terence H. 2000. "Ethics as an Inexact Science: Aristotle's Ambitions for Moral Theory." In *Moral Particularism*, edited by Brad Hooker and Margaret Little, 100–129. Oxford: Oxford University Press.

"Issues." n.d. *The Hunger Project*. www.thp.org/issues/.

Jacobson, Daniel. 2005. "Seeing by Feeling: Virtues, Skills, and Moral Perception." *Ethical Theory and Moral Practice* 8: 387–409.

Jacobson, Kristi, and Lori Silverbush. 2013. *A Place at the Table*. Documentary. Magnolia Pictures.

Kelly, Erin I. 2013. "What Is an Excuse?" In *Blame: Its Nature and Norms*, edited by D. Justin Coates and Neal A. Tognazzini, 244–62. Oxford: Oxford University Press.

Kennedy, Scott Hamilton. 2008. *The Garden*. Documentary. Black Valley Films.

Kenner, Robert. 2008. *Food, Inc.* Documentary. Magnolia Pictures.

Kirkland, Anna. 2011. "The Environmental Account of Obesity: A Case for Feminist Skepticism." *Signs* 36 (2): 463–85.

Knowles, John H. 1977. "The Responsibility of the Individual." In *Doing Better and Feeling Worse: Health in the United States*, edited by John H. Knowles, 57–80. New York: W. W. Norton.

Kohl-Arenas, Erica. 2016. *The Self-Help Myth: How Philanthropy Fails to Alleviate Poverty*. Oakland: University of California Press.

Lance, Mark, and Margaret Little. 2004. "Defeasibility and the Normative Grasp of Context." *Erkenntinis* 61 (2–3): 435–55.

Lance, Mark, and Margaret Little. 2006. "Particularism & Anti-Theory." In *The Oxford Handbook of Ethical Theory*, edited by D. Copp, 567–94. Oxford: Oxford University Press.

Levy, Neil. 2011. "Addiction, Responsibility, and Ego Depletion." In *Addiction and Responsibility*, edited by Jeffrey Poland and George Graham, 89–111. Philosophical Psychopathology: Disorders of the Mind. Cambridge, MA: MIT Press.

Lipman, Matthew. 1983. *Lisa*. Second edition. Montclair, NJ: Institute for the Advancement of Philosophy for Children.

Lipman, Matthew. 1996a. *Deciding What to Do: Instructional Manual to Accompany Nous*. Montclair, NJ: Institute for the Advancement of Philosophy for Children.

Lipman, Matthew. 1996b. *Nous*. Montclair, NJ: Institute for the Advancement of Philosophy for Children.

Lipman, Matthew, Ann Margaret Sharp, and Frederick S. Oscanyan. 1980. *Philosophy in the Classroom*. Second edition. Philadelphia: Temple University Press.

List, Charles. 2013. *Hunting, Fishing, and Environmental Virtue: Reconnecting Sportsmanship and Conservation*. Corvallis: Oregon State University Press.

Little, Margaret Olivia. 2000. "Moral Generalities Revisited." In *Moral Particularism*, edited by Brad Hooker and Margaret Little, 276–304. Oxford: Clarendon Press.

Little, Margaret Olivia. 2001a. "Wittgensteinian Lessons on Moral Particularism." In *Slow Cures and Bad Philosophers: Essays on Wittgenstein, Medicine, and Bioethics*, edited by Carl Elliott, 161–80. Durham and London: Duke University Press.

Little, Margaret Olivia. 2001b. "On Knowing the 'Why': Particularism and Moral Theory." *Hastings Center Report* 31 (4): 32–40.

Little, Margaret Olivia. 2007. "Seeing and Caring: The Role of Affect in Feminist Moral Epistemology." In *Foundations of Ethics: An Anthology*, edited by Russ Shafer-Landau and Terence Cuneo, 420–32. Blackwell Philosophy Anthologies. Malden, MA: Blackwell.

Little, Margaret Olivia, and Brad Hooker, eds. 2000. *Moral Particularism*. Oxford: Clarendon Press.

Lobel, Arnold. 1980. *Fables*. New York: Harper Collins.

Longoria, Eva, and Eric Schlosser. 2014. *Food Chains: The Revolution in America's Fields*. Documentary. Screen Media Films.

Lyons, Pat. 2009. "Prescription for Harm: Diet Industry Influence, Public Health Policy, and the 'Obesity Epidemic.'" In *The Fat Studies Reader*, edited by Esther Rothblum and Sondra Solovay, 75–87. New York: New York University Press.

Matthews, Gareth B. 1994. *The Philosophy of Childhood*. Cambridge, MA: Harvard University Press.

McClintock, Nathan. 2011. "From Industrial Garden to Food Desert: Demarcated Devaluation in the Flatlands of Oakland, California." In *Cultivating Food Justice: Race, Class, and Sustainability*, edited by Alison Hope Alkon and Julian Agyeman, 89–120. Food, Health, and the Environment. Cambridge, MA: MIT Press.

McMillan, Tracie. 2012. *The American Way of Eating: Undercover at Walmart, Applebee's, Farm Fields and the Dinner Table*. New York: Scribner.

McNaughton, David. 1988. *Moral Vision*. Oxford: Blackwell.

Mead, Lawrence M. 2006. *Beyond Entitlement: The Social Obligations of Citizenship*. New York: Free Press.

Meyers, Diana Tietjens. 2004. "Narrative and Moral Life." In *Setting the Moral Compass: Essays by Women Philosophers*, edited by Cheshire Calhoun, 288–305. Studies in Feminist Philosophy. New York: Oxford University Press.

Meyers, Diana Tietjens. 2014. "Rethinking Coercion for a World of Poverty and Transnational Migration." In *Poverty, Agency, and Human Rights*, edited by Diana Tietjens Meyers, 69–91. Oxford: Oxford University Press.

Meyers, Diana Tietjens. 2016. *Victims' Stories and the Advancement of Human Rights*. Oxford: Oxford University Press.

Misak, Cheryl. 2008. "Experience, Narrative, and Ethical Deliberation." *Ethics* 118 (4): 614–32.

Moss, Michael. 2013. *Salt Sugar Fat: How the Food Giants Hooked Us*. New York: Random House.

Murray, Charles. 1984. *Losing Ground: American Social Policy, 1950–1980*. New York: Basic Books.

Nazario, Sonia. 2006. *Enrique's Journey: The Story of a Boy's Dangerous Odyssey to Reunite with His Mother*. New York: Random House.

Nelkin, Dana. 2008. "Responsibility and Rational Abilities: Defending an Asymmetrical View." *Pacific Philosophical Quarterly* 89(4): 497–515.

Nelson, Hilde Lindemann. 2001. *Damaged Identities, Narrative Repair*. Ithaca, NY: Cornell University Press.

Nestle, Marion. 2002. *Food Politics: How the Food Industry Influences Nutrition and Health*. Berkeley: University of California Press.

Nestle, Marion. 2015. *Soda Politics: Taking on Big Soda (and Winning)*. Oxford: Oxford University Press.

Nestle, Marion, and Malden Nesheim. 2012. *Why Calories Count: From Science to Politics*. Berkeley: University of California Press.

Nussbaum, Martha C. 1990. *Love's Knowledge: Essays on Philosophy and Literature*. New York: Oxford University Press.

O'Connor, Anahad. 2016. "Study Tied to Food Industry Tries to Discredit Sugar Guidelines." *New York Times*, December 19. www.nytimes.com/2016/12/19/well/eat/a-food-industry-study-tries-to-discredit-advice-about-sugar.html.

O'Connor, Anahad. 2017. "In the Shopping Cart of a Food Stamp Household: Lots of Soda." *New York Times*, January 13, sec. "Well-Eat." www.nytimes.com/2017/01/13/well/eat/food-stamp-snap-soda.html?action=click&contentCollection=Opinion&module=Trending&version=Full&region=Marginalia&pgtype=article.

"PBIS in the Classroom." 2017. *Positive Behavioral Intervention Services*. March. www.pbis.org/school/pbis-in-the-classroom.

Pheterson, Gail. 1989. *A Vindication of the Rights of Whores*. Seattle, WA: Seal Press.

"Plant a Row for the Hungry." n.d. *Garden Writers Association*. https://gardenwriters.org/Plant-a-Row.

Poland, Jeffrey, and George Graham, eds. 2011. *Addiction and Responsibility*. Philosophical Psychopathology: Disorders of the Mind. Cambridge, MA: MIT Press.

Pollan, Michael. 1991. *Second Nature: A Gardener's Education*. New York: Grove Press.

Pollan, Michael. 2008. *In Defense of Food: An Eater's Manifesto*. New York: Penguin Books.

Poppendieck, Janet. 1998. *Sweet Charity? Emergency Food and the End of Entitlement*. New York: Penguin.

Prager, Michael. 2010. *Fat Boy Thin Man*. Prager: Michael.

Pritchard, Michael. 1996. *Reasonable Children: Moral Education and Moral Learning*. Lawrence: University Press of Kansas.

Reynolds, Kristin, and Nevin Cohen. 2016. *Beyond the Kale: Urban Agriculture and Social Justice Activism in New York City*. Geographies of Justice and Social Transformation. Athens: University of Georgia Press.

Robinson, Jenefer. 2005. *Deeper Than Reason: Emotion and Its Role in Literature, Music, and Art*. Oxford: Clarendon Press.

Sbicca, Joshua. 2012. "Growing Food Justice by Planting an Anti-Oppression Foundation: Opportunities and Obstacles for a Budding Social Movement." *Agriculture and Human Values* 29 (4): 455–66.

Schlosberg, David. 2007. *Defining Environmental Justice: Theories, Movements, and Nature*. Oxford: Oxford University Press.

Schlosser, Eric. 2005. *Fast Food Nation: The Dark Side of the All-American Meal*. New York: HarperPerennial.

Shaw, Randy. 2008. *Beyond the Fields: Cesar Chavez, the UFW, and the Struggle for Justice in the 21st Century*. Berkeley: University of California Press.

Sherman, Nancy. 1989. *The Fabric of Character: Aristotle's Theory of Virtue*. Oxford: Oxford University Press.

Shklar, Judith. 1990. *The Faces of Injustice*. New Haven: Yale University Press.

Singer, Peter, and Jim Mason. 2006. *The Ethics of What We Eat: Why Our Food Choices Matter*. New York: Rodale.

Skurzynski, Gloria. 1980. *Honest Andrew*. New York: Harcourt Brace Jovanovich.

Smith, Angela M. 2013. "Moral Blame and Moral Protest." In *Blame: Its Nature and Norms*, edited by D. Coates and N. Tognazzini, 27–47. Oxford: Oxford University Press.

Soechtig, Stephanie. 2014. *Fed Up*. Documentary. Radius-TWC.

Stichter, Matt. 2007. "Ethical Expertise: The Skill Model of Virtue." *Ethical Theory and Moral Practice* 10 (2): 183–94.

Stichter, Matt. 2011. "Virtues, Skills, and Right Action." *Ethical Theory and Moral Practice* 14: 73–86.

Stolberg, Sheryl G. 2013. "On the Edge of Poverty, at the Center of a Debate on Food Stamps." *New York Times*, September 4.

"Stories of Success." n.d. *The Hunger Project*. www.thp.org/our-work/stories-of-success/.

"Storytelling Project—Turning Anecdotes into Useful Data." n.d. *GobalGiving*. www.globalgiving.org/stories/.

Strawson, Peter F. 1962. "Freedom and Resentment." *Proceedings of the British Academy* 48: 1–25.

Swartwood, Jason. 2012. "Wisdom as an Expert Skill." *Ethical Theory and Moral Practice* (April). doi:10.1007/s10677-012-9367-2.

Taubes, Gary. 2017. "Big Sugar's Secret Ally? Nutritionists." *New York Times*, January 13, sec. "Sunday Review-Opinion." www.nytimes.com/2017/01/13/opinion/sunday/big-sugars-secret-ally-nutritionists.html?action=click&contentCollection=Politics&module=Trending&version=Full&region=Marginalia&pgtype=article.

Taylor, Christopher. 2008. *Food Fight*. Documentary. November Films.

"Tell Stories with Purpose." n.d. *Hatch for Good*. www.hatchforgood.org/?utm_source=rf&utm_medium=blog&utm_campaign=htclaunch.

Vargas, Manuel. 2013a. *Building Better Beings: A Theory of Moral Responsibility*. New York: Oxford University Press.

Vargas, Manuel. 2013b. "Situationism and Moral Responsibility: Free Will in Fragments." In *Decomposing the Will*, edited by Andy Clark, Julian Kiverstein, and Tillman Vierkant, 325–49. Oxford: Oxford University Press.

Veatch, Robert M. 1980. "Voluntary Risks to Health." *Journal of the American Medical Association* 243 (1): 50–55.

Wallace, R. Jay. 1994. *Responsibility and the Moral Sentiments*. Cambridge, MA: Harvard University Press.

Wansik, Brian. 2004. "Environmental Factors That Increase the Food Intake and Consumption Volume of Unknowing Consumers." *Annual Review of Nutrition* 24 (1): 455–79.

Wansik, Brian. 2006. *Mindless Eating: Why We Eat More Than We Think*. New York: Bantam Books.

Waugh, Louisa. 2007. *Selling Olga: Stories of Human Trafficking and Resistance*. London: Orion Books.

"What We Do." n.d. *Mother Hubbard's Cupboard*. http://mhcfoodpantry.org/.

"Who We Are." n.d. *The Hunger Project*. www.thp.org/who-we-are/.

Wikler, Daniel. 1987. "Who Should Be Blamed for Being Sick?" *Health Education Quarterly* 14 (1): 11–25.

Wilkins, Jennifer L. 2005. "Eating Right Here: Moving from Consumer to Food Citizen." *Agriculture and Human Values* 22: 269–73.

Winne, Mark. 2008. *Closing the Food Gap: Resetting the Table in the Land of Plenty*. Boston, MA: Beacon Press.

Winson, Anthony. 2004. "Bringing Political Economy into the Debate on the Obesity Epidemic." *Agriculture and Human Values* 21: 299–312.

Wolf, Aaron. 2007. *King Corn*. Documentary.

Wolf, Susan. 1990. *Freedom within Reason*. New York: Oxford University Press.

Young, Iris Marion. 1990. *Justice and the Politics of Difference*. Princeton: Princeton University Press.

Young, Iris Marion. 2011. *Responsibility for Justice*. Oxford Political Philosophy. Oxford: Oxford University Press.

Zinczenko, David. 2002. "Don't Blame the Eater." *New York Times*, November 23, sec. "Opinion."

Index